Todd France

EYAL PRESS is an author and journalist based in New York. His work has appeared in *The New York Review of Books*, *The New York Times Magazine*, *The Nation*, *Raritan: A Quarterly Review*, and numerous other publications. A 2011 Bernard L. Schwartz fellow at the New America Foundation, he is the author of *Absolute Convictions* and a past recipient of the James Aronson Award for Social Justice Journalism.

ALSO BY EYAL PRESS

Absolute Convictions: My Father, a City, and the Conflict That Divided America

Additional Praise for *Beautiful Souls*

"*Beautiful Souls* gets to the heart of things. . . . Reportage done so well that it becomes literature." —*The Buffalo News*

"A beautifully written book . . . Fascinating." —NPR's *All Things Considered*

"A study in the psychology of dissent, but more explicitly it is a collection of stories very well told, a biography of unlikely courage." —*The New Scientist*

"Remarkable . . . There are no glib explanations in this book, but there is first-class journalism that makes us feel close to these four people, and that makes us wonder: What would we have done if we were in their situation?" —*South Florida Sun-Sentinel*

"Too often we think of courage only as something required to charge into gunfire or scale an icy peak. Eyal Press looks at courage of a different and far more important kind. His examples spread across decades and continents, and he is wise enough to know that it can take as much bravery to defy an unethical corporation as it does to resist a totalitarian regime. This is an important and inspiring book." —Adam Hochschild, author of *To End All Wars* and *King Leopold's Ghost*

"*Beautiful Souls* helps us understand why a minority stands on principle when a majority fails. It's an important book for our time, about conscience, group pressures, ethics, and psyches, and a beautifully crafted one that never falls prey to simple answers about matters of conscience." —Rebecca Solnit, author of *A Paradise Built in Hell*

"Press supports his arguments with numerous psychology and sociology studies. . . . Instructive . . . A smart and subtle work that assays the nature of resistance, of moral courage."

—*The Daily Beast*

"A fascinating examination of courage . . . Press challenges the assumption that it takes an extraordinary individual to perform extraordinary deeds. . . . Rather than dismissing societal values, [these individuals] hold these ideals—brotherhood, unity, diligence—as inviolable. The real question is why the rest of us don't."

—*Booklist*

BEAUTIFUL SOULS

*The Courage
and Conscience of Ordinary People
in Extraordinary Times*

EYAL PRESS

Picador   Farrar, Straus and Giroux   New York

www.picadorusa.com
www.twitter.com/picadorusa • www.facebook.com/picadorusa
picadorbookroom.tumblr.com

Picador® is a U.S. registered trademark and is used by Farrar, Straus and Giroux under
license from Pan Books Limited.

For book club information, please visit www.facebook.com/picadorbookclub or e-mail
marketing@picadorusa.com.

Designed by Abby Kagan

The Library of Congress has cataloged the Farrar, Straus and Giroux edition as follows:

Press, Eyal.
    Beautiful souls : saying no, breaking ranks, and heeding the voice of conscience in
    dark times / Eyal Press.—1st ed.
        p. cm.
    Includes bibliographical references.
    ISBN 978-0-374-14342-8
    1. Conformity. 2. Courage. 3. Conscience. I. Title.
HM1246.P74 2012
179—dc23   2011034961

Picador ISBN 978-1-250-02408-4

First published in the United States by Farrar, Straus and Giroux

First Picador Edition: February 2013

P1

TO MIREILLE

At the center of our moral life and our moral imagination are the great models of resistance: the great stories of those who have said "No."

—SUSAN SONTAG

CONTENTS

BEAUTIFUL SOULS

PROLOGUE

About a mile beyond the main square in the village of Józefów, in eastern Poland, several dozen wooden stakes poke out among the weeds and bushes on a patch of forest strewn with pinecones and covered in velvety green moss. The stakes are nestled in a thicket of pines on the outskirts of the village, across the road from a murky pond. They would be easy to miss, rising a mere foot or two above the ground, but surrounding them is a waist-high band of blue-and-white ribbons festooned around the trunks of some of the neighboring pines. On the still summer day I followed a footpath through the trees to the edge of this ringed enclosure, the forest was eerily quiet, as though in deference to the villagers whose names were listed on the small, mud-stained notices pinned to the wooden stakes. Sheathed in plastic, the notices were inscribed with hexagonal Jewish stars, Hebrew lettering, and a date—13/7/42.

Early that morning in 1942, before daylight broke, Józefów was equally still. Then a convoy of trucks rattled by. They came from Bilgoraj, roughly eighteen miles to the west, carrying the men of Reserve Battalion 101, a division of the German Order Police whose members announced their presence by rousing the village's eighteen hundred Jewish inhabitants from their homes. The villagers were taken to a marketplace, where the male Jews of working age were separated out—they were destined for a labor camp. Most of the others—women, children, elderly people—were driven in trucks to the edge of a path leading into the woods, marched inside in small groups, and forced to lie face down in rows. The soldiers lined up behind them, placed the tips of their carbines at the base of their targets' necks, and, against the wail of screams that soon echoed through the forest, fired. The first shots rang out in the morning and continued into the night, a marathon of murder that left the woods littered with corpses and body parts. In the shade of the pines, skullcaps were torn off heads. Soldiers emerged from the wilderness splattered in blood, pausing for an occasional smoke before circling back with a fresh batch of victims.

In the knapsack that I carried on my own trek into the forest was a copy of the book *Ordinary Men*, by the historian Christopher Browning, a study of the battalion that swept through Józefów that includes a chilling account of the massacre. I'd read the book long before visiting the scene of the crime but the details had stayed with me, both because of something startling it revealed and because of something I remember feeling it had left out, something I wanted to know more about. The startling revelation concerned not the shootings but a moment that preceded them, when the commander of the battalion, Major Wilhelm Trapp, gathered his men in a semicircle to deliver an address. As one might expect, Trapp reminded the soldiers, only a quarter of whom were members of the Nazi Party, that Jews were the enemies of Germany. Then he announced that if any of the older men did not feel up to participating in the operation, they could refrain. There was a pause, and a soldier stepped forward. About a dozen more followed.

It is an arresting moment, a brief but pregnant exchange that upends the notion that the rank-and-file soldiers who took part in the massacre had no alternative but to participate. They did not join the firing squads because they had to. They joined because they chose to, which raises the question of what ultimately drove them to kill. Browning traces the answer to the fear of standing apart from the group: not taking part in the operation meant leaving the "dirty work" to one's comrades and being seen as casting negative judgment on one's nation and peers, something most of the soldiers in the battalion were loath to do, particularly for the sake of people who were, after all, Jews.

But there is another, equally compelling question that has gone comparatively ignored: namely, why a few ordinary men considered Major Trapp's offer and turned in their guns. Why, even in situations of seemingly total conformity, there are always some people who refuse to go along.

This is a book about such nonconformists, about the mystery of what impels people to do something risky and transgressive when thrust into a morally compromising situation: stop, say no, resist. The extreme circumstances that prevailed among the German soldiers tasked with hunting down and murdering Jews in villages such as Józefów during World War II are, fortunately, something most of us can only imagine being caught up in. Yet there is a reason our imaginations are often drawn to such scenarios—why few of us have failed to wonder at some point whether the impulse to refuse would have gripped us if we'd stood in the shoes of ordinary Germans back then, and, if so, whether we would have had the nerve to act on it. Wondering this is not, in fact, a purely speculative exercise, owing to an unresolved tension that runs through most societies, and for that matter most people's minds. We've all arrived at junctures where our deepest principles collide with the loyalties we harbor and the duties we are expected to fulfill, and wrestled with how far to go to keep our consciences clean. As far as necessary to be true to ourselves, a voice inside our heads tells us. But there are other voices that warn against turning on our community, embarrassing our superiors, or endangering our careers and reputations, maybe even our lives and the lives of our family members.

In Hollywood films and the sanctimonious tributes that have grown increasingly common in recent decades, individuals who stand by their convictions at such moments are invariably depicted as heroes. Trees are planted for them at places like the Yad Vashem Memorial Museum in Jerusalem. Politicians salute them for reminding us of "our moral duty to confront evil in all its forms," as George W. Bush stated upon awarding the U.S. Medal of Freedom in 2005 to Paul Rusesabagina, the hotel manager who risked his life to shelter Tutsis during the 1994 Rwandan genocide (and whose story served as the basis of the movie starring Don Cheadle, *Hotel Rwanda*). After a century of horrors fueled by obedience and conformity, who could argue with this? Surely one of the lessons the civilized world learned from the cataclysms of the modern era is that averting one's eyes from blatant wrongdoing is untenable. Yet confronting evil tends to be seen differently when it is being committed in our name—when the perpetrators are not Germans or Rwandans but Americans carrying out abuses at places such as the Abu Ghraib prison in Iraq, a story that came to light after a reservist named Joseph Darby handed a CD full of incriminating photos to the U.S. Army's Criminal Investigation Division in 2004, one year before President Bush honored Paul Rusesabagina. Darby's reward was to be called a traitor and to receive a string of death threats that prompted him to move out of his hometown.

The speed with which people like Darby are ostracized even in democratic societies shows how much easier it is to admire such nonconformists from a distance than up close, when the beliefs being challenged are one's own. It also illustrates how acts of conscience that some view as heroic may strike others as acts of betrayal, subversion, or irresponsibility. This is the fear that stalks the narrator of *Khirbet Khizeh*, a novella published in 1949 that tells the story of an Israeli army unit dispatched on a mission to clear "infiltrators" out of a village during the 1948 Arab-Israeli war. Written by S. Yizhar, the pen name of Yizhar Smilansky, a veteran of that conflict, the novella records the inner torment of a soldier who comes to realize the targets of the operation are unarmed civilians. Ordered to load the village's inhabitants onto trucks and demolish their homes, the soldier balks. "If someone had to get filthy, let others soil their hands," he tells himself. "I couldn't. Absolutely not. But immediately another voice started up inside me singing this song: Bleeding heart, bleeding heart, bleeding heart. With increasing petulance and a psalm to the beautiful soul that left the dirty work to others, sanctimoniously shutting its eyes, averting them so as to save itself from anything that might upset it, with eyes too pure to behold evil." Overcoming his queasiness, the soldier ends up submitting to the order, and is then haunted by the thought that he's colluded in a crime.

What does it take to resist at such moments? And how can we know that we should? Saying no may be appropriate when no reasonable argument can be made for complying, but what about when one can? At what point might an act of principled defiance veer into recklessness—or zealotry? And even if resistance is justified, what beyond keeping the hands of a few upstanding individuals clean does refusal that's not tethered to some larger social objective achieve?

Philosophers and political theorists have devoted much energy to probing such questions, but often at a high level of abstraction and at a great remove from people grappling with particular dilemmas in real time. In part to compensate for this imbalance, I've taken the opposite approach. To understand what leads some people to muster the courage to refuse, I decided I had to meet some of them and learn as much as possible about the details of their lives—lives that fascinate me in part because they never seemed headed for conflict and mutiny. The literature on dissent and disobedience is dominated by stories about rebellious outsiders who challenge authority or convention in order to advance a clearly defined ideological agenda: Marxist revolutionaries, members of the French Resistance, pacifists who burned their draft cards during the Vietnam War. But there is another, less familiar, no less important band of dissenters: insiders who never thought of themselves as part of an opposition movement, who do not have to leap across an abyss to say no to the system, and who end up doing so not because they brazenly rejected its ideals but because, if anything, they believed in those ideals too much.

The stories that follow trace the paths of four such resisters through a variety of fraught circumstances. The narrative begins with a police captain in 1938 who violates the thing he is duty-bound to enforce—the law—at a time when countries throughout the world were crafting rules that left countless officials like him with a choice between doing their jobs or saving innocents. Chapter 2 unfolds in the Balkans half a century later, telling the story of a Serb who crosses the lines of ethnic division that cleaved the former Yugoslavia in the early 1990s. It is about resisting something more amorphous but no less powerful than the law: one's community. Technically speaking, neither of the characters in the first two chapters actually says no: they speak through their actions, doing the opposite of what they are told and dealing with the potentially calamitous consequences they know may befall them. The defiance is more public for the protagonist in the third chapter, a soldier in an elite unit of the Israeli army who decides he doesn't want to serve in the military anymore, but the struggle is more internal. The soldier's story is about what happens when the ideas and assumptions at the core of a person's identity unravel: about saying no to oneself. The final chapter, about a broker who refuses to sell a financial instrument she fears may expose her clients to risk, traces a similar internal struggle, only in an environment where the expectation is not that individuals will sacrifice for their nation or community but that they will look out only for themselves. It is about saying no to greed and apathy, which arguably play more of a role in fostering conformity in our profit-obsessed times than anything else.

Such stories merit attention not only because we live in a world sorely lacking compelling examples of moral courage but also because of something too often lost in contemporary accounts of evil, which is that deciding whether to conform or resist is just that: a choice. In the half century since the publication of Hannah Arendt's *Eichmann in Jerusalem*, much of the writing on evil has focused less on the choices and dilemmas facing individuals than on the power of the situation: the squalid conditions that turned U.S. soldiers into torturers at Abu Ghraib; the totalitarian system that, in Arendt's rendering, led a "terrifyingly normal" bureaucrat like Adolf Eichmann to become a mass murderer without registering the horror of his deeds. The dutiful official who oversaw the logistics of the Final Solution committed his crimes "under circumstances that make it well-nigh impossible for him to know or to feel that he is doing wrong," wrote Arendt of Eichmann. It was the system rather than the man that accounted for the wrongdoing, in other words, an idea that has sunk into popular consciousness and turned the phrase "the banality of evil" into a shorthand explanation for atrocities robotically executed by pliant subordinates in countless other settings.

No one familiar with recent history would deny that situational factors do matter. As we'll see, subtle changes in them can play an important role in the stories of resisters as well. But our fixation on the paper-pushing bureaucrat who thoughtlessly obeys has led us to forget that, as powerfully as circumstances may shape and constrain us, deciding what to believe and how to act remains a matter of considerable discretion. Mass violence itself takes a great deal of thought and planning to carry out: it is not always so humdrum and mundane. So, it follows, does thinking and acting in ways that constitute the best, and arguably the only, rejoinder to the familiar refrain of the obedient underling, "I was just following orders."

Legally and morally, we may all agree that foremost responsibility for blatantly unethical policies should fall on high-ranking officials rather than on their subordinates. There surely are situations where exercising moral responsibility is so risky that expecting many people to do so is naïve. But if no one resists, how can those who passively submit or even actively comply be judged, much less held accountable? How can we respond to members of Reserve Battalion 101 who, in interviews years later, insisted they had strict orders and were merely doing what anyone in their position would have? One way is by recognizing that this wasn't exactly true. At Józefów and elsewhere, the executioners "cannot be absolved by the notion that anyone in the same situation would have done as they did," observed Christopher Browning. "For even among them, some refused to kill and others stopped killing."

It is never easy to say no, particularly in extreme situations, but it is always possible, and so it is necessary to try to understand how and why ordinary women and men sometimes make what is difficult but possible real.

1. DISOBEYING THE LAW

I. Underhanded Practices

One night in November 1938, a fourteen-year-old boy named Erich Billig slipped across the Austrian border into Switzerland. It was, he hoped, the final leg of a hastily arranged journey that had begun ten days earlier, on November 9–10, when Billig and Jews throughout Vienna hid in their apartments or ducked for cover while Nazi storm troopers led a bloody rampage through the streets. In the organized pogrom known as Kristallnacht, which turned Austria's stately capital into a cauldron of terror and violence, hundreds of Jewish shops were vandalized, dozens of temples burned down, and scores of injuries and fatalities recorded. The shattered storefronts and smoldering synagogues left little doubt what the unification of Austria and Germany, which Adolf Hitler had announced before cheering throngs of jubilant supporters in Vienna's Heldenplatz ("Heroes' Square") in March, would mean for Jews. Erich Billig already had a sense. A few months earlier his father had been deported to Dachau, a concentration camp near Munich; his older brother, Herbert, had fled the country after landing on the Gestapo's wanted list, and was now in Zurich. After Kristallnacht,

Billig's mother, Hilde, put her youngest son on a train bound for Altach, a town near the Swiss border, where he holed up in an abandoned shed and pondered how to get to Zurich himself.

There was one problem: Switzerland, like every other country in the world, didn't want to take in masses of Jewish refugees. At the Evian Conference, held at the Hotel Royal on the shores of Lake Geneva in July that same year, representatives from thirty-two countries had gathered to discuss the plight of Jews fleeing Nazi persecution. Expressions of sympathy rained down from the dignitaries; promises to take in more refugees did not. Unlike some countries, including the United States, Switzerland did not have a fixed quota limiting immigration on the basis of nationality. It did have a statute requiring Austrian refugees to secure an entry visa beforehand, which the Swiss consulate in Vienna had been directed to grant only to applicants of "Aryan" ancestry.

Lacking the proper lineage, Billig staked his hopes on finding a more discreet path across the border. One night, he and two other Jews he met in Altach entrusted their fate to an Austrian gendarme who claimed to know of such a route. After pocketing the money they'd pooled, the gendarme led them through a forest to a clearing bordered by a shallow creek, a place known to the villagers on the other side of the border as *le vieux Rhin*. Here, for a brief stretch, the great river that flowed down from the Alps and snaked its way along the Swiss-Austrian border before emptying into Lake Constance tapered off into a narrow, easily passable stream. The gendarme motioned toward it and said, "Okay, there's the border. Now you can go to the other side."

The trio of fugitives waded across the knee-high water and followed a footpath into an open field, moving soundlessly along what they thought was an unobstructed path. They hadn't gone far before the sound of dogs barking pierced the silence, tipping off the guards on duty that night.

Hours later, as morning light filtered through the alder trees and spread over the hills and meadows of the neighboring villages, the Swiss authorities confirmed that Billig lacked an entry visa and sent him back to Austria.

Three months before Erich Billig's thwarted expedition, the chiefs of police from the cantons of Switzerland were summoned to attend a conference on immigration in Bern, the Swiss capital. It took place on August 17, 1938, during a spell of glorious weather, a string of cloudless days ideal for leisurely strolls along the banks of the Aare River, which looped around the peninsula on which Bern's cobbled streets and medieval-style buildings were spread out.

The officials at the conference gathered inside the Bundeshaus, a domed edifice set on a promontory where Heinrich Rothmund, head of the Federal Police for Foreigners, held forth. A tall man with a clean-shaven jaw and neatly trimmed mustache, Rothmund was responsible for refugee policy in a country that had long prided itself on its hospitality to strangers, a tradition dating back to the Protestant Reformation, when French Huguenots had settled in Geneva to escape religious persecution. In more recent times, Switzerland had burnished its reputation for neutrality in part by offering shelter to the victims of conflict in bordering states. Rothmund was not unaware of this heritage. "The asylum tradition of our country is so firmly anchored that not only the Swiss citizen but every office that must deal with an individual refugee case is inclined to accept the person without reservations," he observed at one point. But his tolerance was hedged by other concerns. One of these concerns was *Überfremdung*—"foreign overpopulation," an expression that cropped up with growing frequency as the Great Depression fueled anxiety among Swiss citizens that foreigners might take their jobs. Another was *Verjudung*—"Jewification," which Rothmund, among others, portrayed as a virus that could produce unwelcome side effects if allowed to metastasize and spread. "If we do not want to let a movement that is anti-Semitic and unworthy of our country take legitimate roots here, then we need to fend off the immigration of foreign Jews with all our power," Rothmund warned. "We have not used the foreign registration office to oppose foreign penetration, particularly the Jewification of Switzerland, just to let ourselves be flooded by immigrants today."

As the statement suggests, the custom of welcoming strangers gave way to other priorities as the political skies darkened over Europe during the 1930s, all the more so when Jews began spilling over the Swiss border in unprecedented numbers after Germany's annexation of Austria in March 1938. In the months that followed, even refugees with work permits were picked up in Switzerland for "looking Jewish" and sent back. Yet more and more kept coming, driven by desperate circumstances that, in Bern, elicited little sympathy from the officials on hand. "Can't we close our borders better?" asked the chief of police from Zurich during the conference. They certainly spared no effort to try. To make it easier to pick out and identify "non-Aryan" refugees, the Swiss authorities soon prodded Germany to place a special mark on the papers of Jews, a request the Nazis obliged by stamping their passports with a large red *J*. Meanwhile, under the new policy unanimously adopted at the conference organized by Heinrich Rothmund, anyone who crossed the Swiss border without proper papers after August 19, 1938, was to be denied entry "without exception."

The policy of no exceptions is what prevented Erich Billig from being welcomed after he'd been caught sneaking across the Rhine. It did not prevent Billig from trying again, the very next night, with the help of two Swiss guides who distracted the border guards as he forded the river a second time, then spirited him to a secluded bungalow where he ate, slept, and spread his waterlogged shoes and clothes over a stove to dry. The following morning, Billig squeezed into the back of a truck belonging to the guides, who drew a canvas tarp over him and drove to the city of St. Gallen, twenty miles or so inside Switzerland. They pulled to a stop in front of a building by a church near the center of town, the headquarters of a Jewish relief agency. Billig climbed out of the truck and was taken inside to meet the agency's director, a dapper, bespectacled man named Sidney Dreifuss. Shortly thereafter, an official appeared, dressed in a crisp police uniform and wearing a rimless pince-nez held in place by a thin metal chain tucked behind a pair of ear pads. Billig had never seen such a contraption before and he would not soon forget it, not least because, after interrogating him for several minutes and taking stock of his options, the officer with the peculiar ear pads told him that he could stay.

Paul Grüninger was the commander of the state police in St. Gallen, which is situated in northeast Switzerland, on a plateau between the shores of Lake Constance and the snowcapped peaks of the Appenzell Mountains, the northernmost range of the Alps. He was forty-seven years old at the time he met Erich Billig in the Jewish relief agency, a pale, unprepossessing man with gray-green eyes, pursed lips, and a background bereft of obvious clues as to why he would have put his career at risk by violating the policy formulated at the conference on immigration in Bern, which he'd attended.

Born in 1891, Grüninger was the son of middle-class merchants who ran a small cigar shop in St. Gallen. As a youth, he was a mediocre student but precocious athlete whose proudest accomplishments came not in the classroom but on the soccer field (he would later play on a team that won the Swiss national cup). During World War I, he served in the Swiss Army. Some time later, in 1919, an influential client dropped by his parents' cigar shop and tipped them off that the police in St. Gallen had a vacancy and would soon be looking to hire a lieutenant, a position ideal for a young man of military rank. By this point, Grüninger had obtained a teaching diploma and moved to the neighboring town of Au, where he'd joined the staff of a primary school and met Alice Federer, a colleague to whom he'd gotten engaged. Alice didn't want to live in St. Gallen, but at the urging of his mother, Grüninger applied for the opening in the police department and beat out seventy other candidates for the post.

Shortly after they'd settled in St. Gallen, the newly married couple's first daughter, Ruth, was born. A few years later, in 1925, Grüninger was promoted to police captain, which elevated his stature and responsibilities. He soon found himself handling security for foreign dignitaries who visited the canton, among them Emperor Hirohito. In a photo from this period taken in the town of St. Margrethen on an overcast winter day, Grüninger is standing to the emperor's right with his police hat on and his rimless spectacles in place. His shoulders are square, his expression unsmiling, the lapel on his uniform buttoned to the top. He has the orderly aspect of a midlevel civil servant who might have been taken for a punctilious inspections officer, a dutiful official not inclined to let the large moral questions that would soon begin swirling through the air in Europe interfere with his responsibility to do his job, which had been the case. The canton of St. Gallen, known in the nineteenth century for its flourishing embroidery industry, shared a border with Austria. In 1936, volunteers began passing through it en route to Spain, where they joined the Republican side in the Spanish Civil War. Anarchists, Communists, and writers such as George Orwell and André Malraux flocked to join the struggle against General Francisco Franco, who received his supplies and ammunition from Mussolini's Italy and Hitler's Germany. The network shepherding volunteers across the Swiss border was illegal, however, and Grüninger worked to choke it off, meeting on occasion with Joseph Schreider, a member of the Gestapo, to discuss the matter.

On April 3, 1939, two days after Franco proclaimed victory in Spain and one year after Hitler announced Germany's annexation of Austria, Paul Grüninger stepped into the courtyard of the Convent of St. Gallen and strode toward the gate of the building he normally entered to reach his office on the second floor. A rookie police officer named Anton Schneider was waiting for him there.

"Sir, you no longer have the right to enter these premises," Schneider said. "Really?" replied Grüninger in a bewildered tone, unaware that a report singling him out had been circulating among Swiss officials. Its author was Gustav Studer, a white-haired bureaucrat with dark-framed glasses who, in response to inquiries posed by Heinrich Rothmund about reports that refugees were still getting into St. Gallen, had launched an investigation to determine why the identity papers of so many Jews in Switzerland indicated they'd arrived just before August 19, 1938, when the new restrictions had gone into effect. Under questioning, Sidney Dreifuss, the head of the relief agency to which Erich Billig had been taken, admitted that he'd been directed to falsify the dates of Jews who crossed the border after this date by the police captain who'd shown up at his office that morning—and many other times, it appeared. Hundreds of refugees had been given "special permission" to remain in Switzerland, Studer's report indicated, and the person responsible was Paul Grüninger.

The target of Studer's investigation was soon ordered to turn in his uniform. A month later, Grüninger was dismissed and informed that a criminal investigation was under way. In the fall of 1940, he appeared before a panel of judges, who convicted him of violating his oath and arranging for the papers of twenty-one refugees who'd entered Switzerland illegally to be falsified; 118 questionnaires had also been doctored.

"Such underhanded practices threaten the necessary trust and the respectability of authorities and the reliability of subordinates," the court stated, imposing a fine of 300 Swiss francs and an additional 1,013 francs to cover the costs of the investigation. Grüninger did not appeal the ruling, perhaps because, if anything, it understated the extent of his lawbreaking.

Many years later, a patrolman who'd policed the same stretch of the Swiss-Austrian border voiced the sentiment most officials shared about his captain. "In my eyes, he broke the law," the patrolman said of Grüninger. "If an official is an official, he cannot simply act according to his own opinion. Had we had only people like Grüninger from Basel up to Martinsbrugg, I don't know what the Swiss people would have said."

As indelicate as the sentiment may seem, the patrolman was right to wonder what people would have said. Irrespective of its consequences, a law had been enacted, and good citizens in orderly Switzerland obeyed the rules. Truth be told, when it came to refugees fleeing Nazi terror, the orderly Swiss were not alone. "You are a consular officer, in the early years of a diplomatic career that you hope will lead to an ambassadorship," the diplomat Richard Holbrooke has written. "On your desk sit two rubber stamps. Use the one that says 'APPROVED,' and the person in front of you can travel to your country . . . Use the other stamp which says 'REJECTED,' and the visa applicant in front of you might die or go to prison—simply because he or she is Jewish." Between passage of the Nuremberg Laws and the end of World War II, countless officials manning checkpoints, consulates, and border posts faced a version of this dilemma. The choice before them was not an easy one. As Holbrooke noted, "Government service is based on the well-founded principle that officials must carry out their instructions; otherwise, anarchy would prevail." Many of the diplomats in question were low and midlevel officials entrusted to enforce rules that, in democracies such as Switzerland and the United States, carried a presumption of legitimacy, having been enacted by freely elected governments. On the other hand, this also meant that refusing to enforce the laws barring refugees would not likely have endangered their lives, and might even have persuaded their superiors to reconsider whether the statute or policy in question was just. Few deigned to find out. "We heard, and mocked, the defense of many Germans after World War II; they were just following orders," wrote Holbrooke. "But the same rationale was used by the majority of non-German diplomats in Europe."

What possessed Paul Grüninger to take a risk most officials in his shoes scrupulously avoided? One morning, I took a train from Zurich to Heerbrugg, a sleepy town on the border with Austria, to meet someone I thought might know. Shortly after I arrived at the station, an elderly woman appeared on the opposite end of the platform, inching toward me at a gingerly pace with the Welsh terrier she'd told me she'd be tugging along on a leash. The woman's name was Ruth Rudoner. She was small and stooped, with a maze of wrinkles etched around her mouth and gray hair that fell in bangs above her pale gray-green eyes—her father's eyes.

Ruth Rudoner was Paul Grüninger's daughter. She was eighty-seven years old and lived in an apartment a few blocks from the station, to which we slowly made our way with her terrier in the lead. Ruth's home was plainly furnished and slightly musty, with a large maple-colored wood chest, a stuffed gray couch, and white walls adorned with anodyne landscape paintings. She brought out a pot of coffee and, after setting two cups on a tray, began talking about her father, who went from being a respectable authority figure to a covert document falsifier when she was seventeen. I'd come to Heerbrugg hoping Ruth could shed some light on what led her father to undergo this transformation—what set him apart from his peers. Not a lot, she insisted while sipping her coffee. Her father was a "normal" man who liked to take her hiking on weekends and to spend Sundays playing soccer with his friends, she told me. He sang in a church choir and enjoyed playing the piano. He read his fair share, though not in a way that would have led anyone to mistake him for a subversive. He was on friendly terms with one such person—a fiery trade unionist from St. Gallen named Valentin Keel, who was the only socialist to serve as a state deputy in the otherwise conservative canton. Her father cut a more discreet profile, Ruth indicated. A member of the center-right Swiss Radical Party, he kept his nose out of controversy and his political opinions to himself. "He was interested in what was going on, but that's all," she said.

Perhaps her father was guided not by politics but by faith, I thought. In my mind was the story of another wayward official, a Portuguese consul-general named Aristides de Sousa Mendes, who in 1940, while stationed in Bordeaux, began handing out transit visas to Jews running out of places to hide as Nazi forces stormed across Belgium, Holland, and France, in direct defiance of Portugal's ruler, António de Oliveira Salazar, who'd made it clear that accommodating refugees was forbidden. Recalled and dismissed on the grounds that "a civil servant is not competent to question orders which he must obey," Mendes, a devout Catholic, was unrepentant, declaring, "If I am disobeying orders, I'd rather be with God against men than with men against God." Given Grüninger's membership in a church choir and the fact that St. Gallen was home to one of the oldest monasteries in Europe (the city was named after an itinerant monk who'd wandered through the surrounding countryside and settled there in the seventh century), I wondered if Ruth's father might have been cut from similar cloth. "We were Protestant," she told me, but added that, beyond the occasional trip to church, expressions of piety in her family were rare. "Again," she said, "we were normal."

In the literature on the Holocaust, the outliers who refused to become passive bystanders have often been divided into two camps: rescuers who helped Jews out of a basic sense of humanity, and resisters who were driven by ideology. The former were altruists who acted to save lives, the latter political activists committed to the antifascist struggle. Advancing this idealistic struggle is clearly not what drove Paul Grüninger. Could it be that what motivated him was his outsized compassion—a rare sensitivity to suffering that others lacked? Ruth Rudoner's soft voice and gracious manner made me wonder about this. She expressed no bitterness about what had happened to her father, whom she described as a fair-minded, gentle-spirited man. Certainly the record suggested as much—part of the record, at least. A few days before coming to Heerbrugg, I'd met with Stefan Keller, a Swiss journalist and historian who'd written a book about a witch hunt that had unfolded in a village near St. Gallen before World War II. Its targets were an Austrian servant and a Swiss ranger from a prominent local family who fell in love, touching off a scandal worthy of Hawthorne. The lovers were interrogated and confined to psychiatric wards; the servant was eventually lobotomized and then mysteriously disappeared. Nobody felt terribly moved by her plight, including Paul Grüninger. "It was this very narrow village mentality," Keller told me. "Grüninger didn't have much to do with it, but nobody said, This is wrong. The police just did what the authorities told them."

The unfavorable impression Keller took away from his research was still with him when, some time later, he started digging through the Swiss archives to find out whether, as had long been rumored, the police captain who'd presided over this regrettable affair had allowed Jews into Switzerland in 1938 not because of high-minded principles but for less lofty reasons—in particular, money and sexual favors. Far from dismissing these accusations out of hand, Keller told me he suspected they were true, not least because it was well known that many of the smugglers who helped Jews cross the Swiss border illegally did demand compensation for their services, which is hardly surprising in light of how risky doing so was.

Unfortunately for Keller, many of the files in the Swiss archives turned out to be missing. Then it occurred to him that some of the refugees Grüninger had helped might still be alive. He soon tracked down one of them in Brussels, a woman named Klara Hochberg who appeared in a file sprinkled with hazy allusions to sexual improprieties. She'd kissed Grüninger on the cheek one time; he'd later asked after her. When Keller broached the subject of whether Grüninger had taken advantage of her, shame and embarrassment had spread across her face. "I've slept with one man my entire life—this is my husband!" he recalled her telling him indignantly. "It was absolutely scandalous to her," he said. Keller located dozens of other former refugees who'd had encounters with Grüninger. All told him the same thing: that the police captain from St. Gallen had demanded nothing of them.

Keller ended up publishing his findings in a book, *Délit d'humanité: l'affaire Grüninger*, which documented what he'd come to view as the real scandal: that a man who'd refused to carry out a policy many Swiss citizens looked back on with shame had lost his job and never received an official apology. Grüninger's fall from grace was indeed swift and dramatic, a steep downward slide that took him from the company of foreign dignitaries to the cusp of poverty virtually overnight. In August 1939, a few months after he'd been suspended from his job, ordered to hand over his uniform, and subjected to a psychological examination to determine whether he might be deranged (the doctor who examined him could find no evidence of this), he applied for a license to open a pawnshop. The application was turned down. He was denied some of his retirement benefits. He was too proud to ask for handouts, but a disgraced police captain dogged by rumors of corruption had predictably few employment prospects. Grüninger took to working various odd jobs, peddling raincoats, greeting cards, even animal feed at one point. Although some Swiss Jews lent him money behind the scenes, most were careful to distance themselves from a man who threatened to tarnish their own status as upstanding citizens who abided by the rules. (Before Grüninger's dismissal, some Swiss Jews had actually complained that the border in St. Gallen was "too open to undesirable elements." Others worried that the presence of too many refugees might spark an anti-Semitic backlash.)

Lacking a steady income, Grüninger and his wife moved out of the elegant white house with forest-green shutters where they'd lived in St. Gallen and returned to Au, moving in with Alice's parents to avoid paying rent. In later years, he could be spotted on occasion at a local restaurant owned by an acquaintance of his, sipping cider and munching on peanuts, among the cheapest items on the menu.

Paul Grüninger died in 1972, having spent three decades searching in vain for steady employment while failing to disentangle himself from the web of rumors that clung to his name long after he passed away, including whispers that he'd pursued improper relations not only with refugees but also with some of their tormentors. These allegations were spread by the St. Gallen police, who, after Grüninger's conviction, arranged to have his phone tapped and tasked undercover agents to tail him to such shady functions as card games. A police report subsequently raised questions about his "ambiguous financial situation," another about his alleged habit of "boasting of his contacts with foreign authorities, and even with Gestapo officials." The publication of Stefan Keller's book put these allegations to rest, revealing that the target of the smears was put on a Gestapo blacklist after the Germans discovered he had helped some refugees transfer money to Switzerland. Grüninger also sent letters to and authorized entry permits for several prisoners in Dachau whose relatives had made it across the border. In his book, Keller refrained from speculating about what motivated this conservative, seemingly risk-averse police captain to go to such lengths. But he did develop a theory about it. An oppositional temper is clearly not what distinguished Grüninger, Keller told me. Something else did. "You know, from the perspective of the Swiss bureau administration, Grüninger made a big mistake," he said. "He had no barriers. Refugees came to him, right up to the door of his office, sometimes on their knees, and asked for help. He did nothing to separate himself from the people.

"The other police chiefs didn't do this. They delegated. They made the decisions, and delegated the responsibility to others."

II. Mechanisms of Denial

In 1989, a Polish sociologist named Zygmunt Bauman published a book titled *Modernity and the Holocaust*. Dedicated to his wife, Janina, a survivor of the Warsaw Ghetto, the book sought to explain how a nation of civilized, law-abiding "men in uniforms" who loved their families and were often compassionate to their neighbors nevertheless managed to preside over mass murder. An earlier generation of social scientists had traced the answer to the peculiarities of German character—conventionalism, submissiveness, ethnocentrism, and other proto-fascist traits catalogued in studies such as *The Authoritarian Personality*, an influential 1950 book co-authored by the Frankfurt School philosopher Theodor Adorno. Bauman argued that the focus on these personality traits obscured the social and institutional arrangements that made it frighteningly easy for citizens not only in Nazi Germany but in all modern states to transgress the boundaries of conventional morality—to perpetrate crimes they would never dream of committing in their private lives—without feeling responsible for their acts. What made this possible was one of the most celebrated achievements of modernity, he claimed, the emergence of bureaucratic organizations guided by instrumental rationality that turned individuals into specialized functionaries who were trained to focus narrowly on "the job to be done" while putting their moral concerns aside.

"Cruelty correlates with certain patterns of social interaction much more closely than it does with personality features," argued Bauman. Though clearly influenced by Hannah Arendt, whose portrait of Adolf Eichmann as a middling bureaucrat presaged his description of the Nazis as "ordinary people like you and me," in his analysis of obedience Bauman drew most explicitly on the work of another close student of the subject, the social psychologist Stanley Milgram. In 1961, Milgram oversaw an experiment in which an instructor in a gray lab coat ordered a volunteer to press a switch on an electric generator every time another volunteer gave the wrong answer on a paired-word test. The purpose of the experiment was to clarify whether punishment induces people to learn more effectively, the instructor explained, not revealing that the volunteer taking the test was an actor and that the real point was to see whether subjects would obey. Before carrying out the experiment, Milgram figured most people would stop administering shocks once the actor exhibited discomfort and asked to be released. So did a number of psychiatrists whose opinions he sampled. They were wrong. Despite the shrieks and screams that soon echoed through the laboratory at Yale University where the experiment was conducted, 65 percent of participants continued pulling switches until the electricity generator had reached maximum level and the actor had pretended to pass out.

It was a startling display of how quickly ordinary people prodded by an authority figure could be turned into brutal sadists, not in Nazi Germany but among a random sample of accountants, factory workers, clerks, and advertising executives in the United States. Yet as Milgram himself would subsequently note, a penchant for brutality is not what accounted for the distressingly high rate of obedience. As the experiment unfolded, most of the volunteers in the lab protested. Not a few begged for it to stop. "He's in there hollering!" exclaimed a participant named Fred Ponzi. "I'm not going to kill that man." At this point, the experimenter explained that he, not the volunteer, would be responsible if anything went awry. "You accept all responsibility?" Ponzi asked. "The responsibility is mine . . . Please go on," the instructor assured him. And go on Ponzi did. What happened at such moments was that the volunteer entered what Milgram termed the "agentic state," whereby an individual "sees himself as an agent for carrying out another person's wishes" and stops agonizing about the consequences. "Any force or event that is placed between the subject and the consequences of shocking the victim will lead to a reduction of strain on the participant and thus lessen disobedience," Milgram observed. "In modern society others often stand between us and the final destructive act to which we may contribute."

Here was the essence of modern bureaucracy, Bauman warned: the high-ranking officials who formulated criminal policies delegated responsibility to subordinates and didn't have to see the consequences. The subordinates implementing their decisions could tell themselves, rightly, that they were merely acting at their superiors' behest, and so went about focusing on their discrete jobs. Responsibility thus became "unpinnable," which is how a group of decent, even kindhearted adults could preside over an unconscionable endeavor without losing a second of sleep.

It was a deeply unsettling theory. But it rested on a premise that was arguably not so bleak, which is that individuals followed unjust laws and orders mainly because they were put in situations that "spared [them] the agony of witnessing the outcome" of their deeds, as Bauman put it. Inhumanity was not necessarily a product of willful aggression or hateful ideas, in other words. More often than not, it was a product of disavowal and distance. "Perhaps the most striking among Milgram's findings is the inverse ratio of readiness to cruelty and proximity to its victims," noted Bauman. This is indeed what Milgram deduced. In his original experiment, the learner had been seated behind a glass panel in a separate room. "It's funny how you really begin to forget that there's a guy out there, even though you can hear him," one subject told him afterward. "For a long time I just concentrated on pressing the switches and reading the words." Such comments led Milgram to wonder what might happen if the arrangements were altered slightly so that the victim intruded more on the subject's awareness. He therefore repeated the experiment with the learner and volunteer in the same room. The percentage of defiant subjects promptly doubled, from around one-third to 60 percent.

"The mechanism of denial can no longer be brought into play," Milgram observed. In another variation, the learner received an electric jolt only when his hand rested on a shock plate; at 150 volts, he pulled his hand away. At this point, the instructor ordered the volunteer to force the hand back in place. Seventy percent of participants refused. Observing the pattern, Milgram concluded that the capacity to disobey had a great deal to do with a person's proximity to the harm and with how directly responsible for it he or she felt.

Not long after visiting the archives at Yale to examine the papers of Stanley Milgram, I came upon a book by one of his students,

Eva Fogelman's *Conscience and Courage*, a study of ordinary people who defied authority and in some cases broke the law to rescue Jews during World War II—people like Paul Grüninger. "Milgram's was the first psychological explanation of how—and why— good, decent people could carry out horrendous deeds," Fogelman wrote in her introduction. "What caught my attention, however, were not those who obeyed authority, but those who did not." In the book, Fogelman told the story of an Italian man named Giorgio Perlasca who was walking through the streets of Budapest one day when he paused suddenly. A group of Nazis had chased down a young boy and were assaulting him in broad daylight. As Perlasca watched, one of the Germans bashed the boy's head with a gun. Perlasca asked another witness what the victim had done to provoke them. Nothing, he was told—he was simply Jewish. Perlasca was appalled, and after witnessing this attack committed his life to rescuing Jews, a reaction that would not have been obvious from his background. The Budapest representative of a company that supplied meat to the Italian navy, he had fought with the Italian army in the Spanish Civil War—on the side of General Franco.

As the story indicates, admirable politics and impeccable moral credentials were not traits that united Fogelman's subjects, a motley crew that included not only erstwhile Franco sympathizers but also "sneaks, thieves, smugglers, hijackers, blackmailers, and killers." One characteristic they did share was a level of awareness that made it hard for them to put the faces of the victims out of mind. More often than not, Fogelman found, this awareness was spurred not by abstract principles or distinctive personality traits but by a searing personal experience: in some cases, what psychologists call a "transforming encounter" like the one Giorgio Perlasca underwent; in others, a more gradual accumulation of "influences and events" that eventually triggered an awakening.

As Stefan Keller had told me, most of the police captains in Switzerland took pains to avoid such encounters by delegating tasks to their subordinates and limiting face-to-face contact with refugees.

Paul Grüninger didn't. Every day, refugees showed up at his office begging to stay in Switzerland. Every week, he witnessed scenes that made it resoundingly clear what enforcing the new policy would mean. On one occasion, he was called to the border because the guards didn't know what to do with an elderly man who was threatening to jump into the Rhine if deported. On another, three young Jews insisted they'd be shot if expelled. Although it would be a few more years before the Nazis started systematically exterminating Jews in concentration camps, by the spring of 1938 any official in Switzerland who bothered to read the newspapers knew unsettling scenes like this were occurring with growing regularity, as Hitler set about making the German Reich *Judenrein*—"cleansed of Jews." ("The approximately 500,000 Jews still remaining in Germany are supposed to be expelled somehow," the Swiss foreign envoy in Paris reported after speaking with the German secretary of state, Ernst von Weizsäcker, in 1938. "If, as has been the case up to now, no country is willing to accept them, they face extermination in the short or long term.") But as Ruth Rudoner reminded me, hearing about the Nazis' agenda was not the same thing as witnessing the situation up close. The officials in Bern who formulated the refugee policy "didn't see the people, so it was easy for them to do that," she told me. Her father lacked the same mechanism of denial, which is why he couldn't bring himself to enforce the law.

"He saw what condition the people were in when they arrived and he knew all too well what would happen if he sent them back," she said. "He would always say, 'I could do nothing else.'"

III. Choices and Beliefs

On April 5, 1939, Paul Grüninger wrote a letter to the Swiss government defending his conduct in which he portrayed himself as, in effect, a victim of circumstance. "Whoever had the opportunity, as I had, to repeatedly witness the heartbreaking scenes of the people concerned, the screaming and crying of mothers and children, the threats and suicide and attempts to do it, could . . . ultimately not bear it anymore," Grüninger averred.

A few years later, in 1942, some of Grüninger's former colleagues did get such an opportunity, while inspecting locations along the Swiss border with France. The expedition had been organized by Heinrich Rothmund, the man who'd orchestrated Grüninger's dismissal and who was now worried that the supposedly watertight border was springing new leaks. He was right to be worried. No sooner had the officials left a border post near Grandfontaine than word arrived that five Jewish refugees had turned up there. Soon fifteen more showed up in nearby Boncourt. The officials and border guards rushed to round up the culprits—Belgian Jews, Polish Jews, a mother with a child whose husband was already in Switzerland, another young child. But they did not deport them. "I thought about instructing the guards to expel them," Rothmund later informed a colleague of his. "However, I didn't want to make a hasty decision, and frankly, I did not have the heart to expel them since there were two cute children, and I did believe that their lives would have been in danger if I had done so."

The story appears to illustrate exactly what Grüninger claimed: that anyone who saw what he did would have done the same thing, even the official who'd designed the policy of deportation. That, moreover, what ultimately determines moral conduct are not character traits, personal beliefs, or political attitudes but situational factors, as not a few social psychologists and philosophers have indeed come to believe. "Studies designed to test whether people behave differently in ways that might reflect their having different character traits have failed to find relevant differences," the philosopher Gilbert Harman has argued. "It may even be the case that there is no such thing as character." Among the studies lending support to this view is an experiment designed by John Darley and Bibb Latané that sought to determine what led bystanders to help a stranger in an emergency—in the case of their experiment, an epileptic seizure heard over an intercom. Personality traits (tender-heartedness, coldness) turned out to matter little. The key factor was whether the bystander believed he or she alone heard the attack or thought other people were present, in which case the likelihood of intervention declined, a phenomenon Darley and Latané termed "the diffusion of responsibility."

For a brief moment in Boncourt, Heinrich Rothmund felt the responsibility for the survival of several families was his, and so he had a change of heart. But only very briefly, it turned out. On the same day that Rothmund wrote to his colleague about the refugees he couldn't bring himself to expel, he managed to block out their image long enough to arrange for the border restrictions to be tightened anew. He also took pains to avoid visiting the checkpoints again. "As soon as Rothmund sat at his desk in Bern again, the faces of the people paled, displaced by 'fears of excessive foreignization' and the fear of 'excessive Jewish influence' in Switzerland," noted the Independent Commission of Experts in its official report on Swiss refugee policy during World War II.

As Rothmund's conduct showed, human beings don't inflict harm on others merely because layers of bureaucracy or physical distance lead them to stop thinking about the consequences of their actions. Often they do so because of a factor conspicuously absent from the artificial experiment Stanley Milgram designed: ideological convictions and beliefs. In other words, because they believe the harsh policy they're enforcing is justified, even moral. So it was with another bureaucrat operating in a very different context, Adolf Eichmann, who was not quite the robotic functionary Hannah Arendt portrayed him to be—who, indeed, repeatedly went out of his way to ensure that the number of Jews excluded from deportations to the camps was minimized, even though he'd witnessed his share of heartbreaking scenes. One time Eichmann watched German soldiers slaughter scores of naked Jews standing on the edge of a pit. "There were children in that pit. I saw a woman hold a child of a year or two in the air, pleading," he later recalled.

"At that moment, I wanted to say 'Don't shoot, hand over the child.'" As the statement suggests, Eichmann was not actually incapable of knowing and feeling that murdering innocent people was wrong. Yet he got over his misgivings quickly enough, not because the victims were an abstraction to him but because he was a committed Nazi and ardent anti-Semite who, in the end, decided it was more important to serve his nation and party.

In his study of Reserve Battalion 101, the unit of German soldiers that carried out the massacre in Józefów and countless other atrocities during World War II, Christopher Browning drew directly on Stanley Milgram's experiment on obedience to explain why some conscripts refrained from participating in specific operations. In some massacres and "Jew hunts" where the soldiers saw their victims and the killing was personal, individual policemen refused to fire. When they were assigned to herd throngs of anonymous deportees onto trains en masse (operations that killed far more people), by contrast, everything went off smoothly. "Direct proximity to the horror of the killing significantly increased the number of men who would no longer comply," Browning observed.

Nevertheless, in places like Józefów, where the faces and screams of the victims were all too easy to see and hear, most of the battalion's members still did comply, and one of the reasons was surely that, unlike the subjects in Milgram's laboratory, they didn't view the people they were harming as fellow volunteers in an educational experiment. They saw them as members of a dehumanized minority group that had to be eliminated for the good of the Fatherland. Daniel Goldhagen's theory that Germans were gripped by a uniquely virulent brand of "eliminationist" anti-Semitism, which predated Hitler's rise to power and led them to kill Jews with exuberant joy, has rightly been criticized as simplistic and crude. But few scholars would deny that pervasive anti-Semitism did play a powerful role in fostering brutality and turning many Germans into "willing executioners." "The men of Reserve Battalion 101, like the rest of German society, were immersed in a deluge of racist and anti-Semitic propaganda," observed Browning. Although most were not members of the Nazi Party, many referred to Jews as "dirty," "unkempt," "less clean." Some clearly relished tormenting them—Sergeant Heinrich Bekemeier, for example, a sadistic Nazi who on one occasion responded to an elderly Jewish man who begged him for mercy by shooting him in the mouth.

Proximity can easily be overcome by indoctrination, a lesson not only the Nazis understood. During World War II, a study by a team of U.S. researchers found that no more than 15 to 20 percent of American infantry soldiers on the front lines actually shot at the enemy. "The average and normally healthy individual—the man who can endure the mental and physical stresses of combat—still has such an inner and usually unrealized resistance toward killing a fellow man that he will not of his own volition take life if it is possible to turn away from that responsibility," Brigadier General S.L.A. Marshall, the lead author of the study, concluded. "At the vital point, he becomes a conscientious objector." In the decades that followed, the U.S. Army set about changing this, both by training soldiers to fire reflexively at "pop-up" targets and by convincing them that their opponents were not people but "inferior forms of life," as Lieutenant Colonel Dave Grossman, a former professor of psychology at West Point, has observed. The creation of such "cultural" and "moral" distance reached its peak at places such as My Lai during the Vietnam War, when U.S. soldiers took aim at "gooks," "Commies," "rats," "Charlie"—and where the firing rate rose to 90 percent.

Officials in Switzerland during World War II were not subjected to the relentless racism that shaped the moral atmosphere in Nazi Germany. Many took pride in their nation's tolerance. Yet lurking in the air was the fear of "foreign overpopulation," and the related threat of "Jewification." Being stationed near the border didn't always soften such attitudes; sometimes it hardened them. "Border guards relentlessly sent back illegal refugees almost everywhere, often turning them over directly to the German police, in full knowledge of the danger that threatened them," observed the Swiss Commission of Experts in its report. "At the same time, a process of brutalization occurred. Border guards hit refugees with their rifle butts to prevent them from crossing the border."

"I could do nothing else": the phrase Ruth Rudoner recalled her father voicing does not quite mesh with these facts. The words sound weirdly like those of a man submitting to a stern authority figure, and, in a way, Grüninger was—the sway of his conscience, his inner voice, which made him feel that letting in refugees was his only choice. But in fact there were other choices, plenty of them. In the letter he wrote defending his conduct, Grüninger indeed justified the one he made. He could have felt the flicker of conscience, gone home, mulled the risks of violating the law, and decided he'd best avoid venturing near the border again. He could have slipped into the "agentic state," passing responsibility for the policy up the chain of command, to Heinrich Rothmund. He could have become hardened or brutalized. Or, short of this, taken comfort in the thought that, even if sealing the border was a bit cruel, preventing "excessive Jewish influence" from tainting Switzerland made it necessary.

Why didn't he? The answer is that preventing this was not a priority of his, owing to a trait that was not so normal. In a part of Switzerland where nearly everyone was either Catholic or Protestant and the token Jewish presence had sparked its share of bigotry—in the 1920s, a Christian defense group waged an anti-Semitic campaign against Jews on the St. Gallen City Council—Grüninger failed to exhibit even a trace of anti-Semitic bias, much to Stefan Keller's surprise. "I never found a word written by Grüninger against Jews," Keller told me. "Even among people who helped Jews, you always find a bit of anti-Semitic remarks from this time. I was astonished."

Conventional in his political attitudes, Paul Grüninger was

unconventionally tolerant, which shaped what he saw when he came into contact with refugees—not "Jews" or "foreigners" but "people who had been horribly mistreated," as he put it in a statement defending his conduct—and, in turn, how he chose to respond to them. "Perhaps Grüninger forgot that one should be anti-Semitic in Switzerland," said Keller. "But I don't think he thought at this level. He just saw what was happening and he said, 'In this situation we can't send people back.'"

We can't send them back, Grüninger thought, because of another belief to which he fervently adhered. In the arc of his story there is one unbroken thread: his unshakable conviction that Switzerland was the enlightened nation it claimed to be, a sanctuary whose citizens had always extended a welcoming hand to castoffs from more troubled lands. A cynic might have told him that the reality was more complicated—that pursuing a policy of neutrality during World War II would lead to plenty of unenlightened conduct, like depositing Nazi gold into cosseted bank accounts while leaving Hitler's victims brutally exposed. But Grüninger would have waved the cynic off. Not infrequently in 1938, before the conference on immigration in Bern that year, he would drive to Diepoldsau, a small village near the Austrian border where a former embroidery factory had been converted into a makeshift refugee camp. Inside its crowded barracks, hundreds of newly arrived Jews slept on narrow cots arranged in uniform rows. Outside, above the entrance, a white sign with dark trim and black lettering had been mounted: "Dank dem Schweizervolk" ("Thanks to the Swiss People"). Grüninger was touched by this message, not only because he could see the gratitude in the eyes of the residents but also because, in his own eyes, a proud tradition was being upheld.

Later, in seeking to explain his conduct, Grüninger composed a letter citing a speech that a Swiss foreign minister had made in the 1880s about how welcoming strangers was an integral part of Swiss identity and always would be. He never wavered from this starry-eyed view. "Cheer up," he once told a young Jewish girl who arrived at the border with her family in tears, "now you are in free Switzerland"—words that, to Stefan Keller, sound almost touchingly naïve. "This self-constructed image of Switzerland as the country where people are safe, this mythology, it has nothing to do with reality," Keller said. "But Grüninger really believed in it."

To disobey authority requires being rebellious, common sense suggests. Sometimes, though, it is precisely a faithful insider's nonrebelliousness—the earnest belief in Switzerland's asylum tradition, in the justness of its laws—that can spark disobedience. Grüninger was not a rebel but a true believer, a conservative, patriotic man who subscribed wholeheartedly to the tenets of a belief system that his subsequent downfall indeed revealed to be a myth. His conduct was "guided by the opinion of a large part of the Swiss population, the press, and the political parties," he claimed, the forces that rewarded his faith by maintaining their silence as his reputation was blackened for having violated a policy that roused little opposition from his fellow citizens and peers.

Little open opposition, that is.

IV. Correcting Mistakes

"We have ascertained that the cantonal police in St. Gallen is implicated in recent illegal attempts to enter Switzerland." So relayed a report from the border surveillance command in December 1938, a few months before the investigation into Paul Grüninger's misdeeds began. It was drawn up and circulated shortly after several smugglers had been spotted outside a restaurant in Bregenz, Austria. The owner of the restaurant was a taxi driver who had assisted partisans in the antifascist struggle in Spain. The men milling around turned out to be members of a network formed by Swiss socialists to help their Austrian comrades escape the clutches of the Nazis. After being interrogated by the Gestapo, the smugglers were sent back to Switzerland, where, under questioning, they informed the authorities that an official from St. Gallen knew what they were doing and approved of it.

The official in question was not Paul Grüninger. It was Valentin Keel, the former trade unionist who Ruth Rudoner had mentioned to me. Before entering politics and becoming a state deputy, Keel had served as the editor of a leftist newspaper that routinely hurled salvos at the authorities. In a conservative canton, he had a reputation as a firebrand, an outspoken antifascist who at one point demanded the names of all Swiss officials on the far right who'd pledged their support to Hitler. In January 1939, after the report on illegal attempts to enter Switzerland had circulated, Keel was called to Bern to see Heinrich Rothmund. A week later, he sent a letter to Paul Grüninger explaining that the federal authorities were concerned about the "surprising proportions" of Jewish refugees entering St. Gallen.

If the authorities were surprised, Keel surely wasn't: his office was located directly across the hall from Grüninger's. Every day, he saw Jewish refugees come to Grüninger's door. The two men even lived on the same street, and were on friendly terms, with Keel dropping by on occasion in the company of his granddaughter. Like Grüninger, Keel had attended the immigration conference in Bern. The idea that he was unaware of Grüninger's activities defies plausibility, not least since one of his responsibilities was to oversee the police department.

Grüninger insisted that Keel knew everything, which, if true, makes his own conduct somewhat easier to comprehend. As common sense suggests and experience confirms, it is exceedingly difficult to disobey authority alone, far less so when one feels supported by others. In one variation of his shock experiment, Stanley Milgram demonstrated this by placing the teacher in a room with two peers who were actors and who, at a certain point, disobeyed the order to administer more shocks. Under these conditions, 90 percent of the subjects also disobeyed. "The mutual support provided by men for each other is the strongest bulwark we have against the excesses of authority," Milgram concluded.

"Wenns mi butzt, butzt au de Keel"—"If I go down, so will Keel," Grüninger vowed. Yet it was Keel who, under pressure from Heinrich Rothmund, tapped Gustav Studer to probe Grüninger's misconduct. On March 1, 1939, Keel was called before the State Council to explain what he knew. He could have defended his colleague, perhaps even delivered a speech calling for the restrictions on immigration to be overturned. Instead, facing accusations from the far right that he'd supplied his comrades with passports in the midst of a bruising reelection campaign, Keel admitted to knowing that a handful of socialists had been spirited across the border, but claimed ignorance of Grüninger's activities. Sidney Dreifuss, of the Jewish Aid to Refugees Office in St. Gallen, told investigators he had no choice but to submit to Grüninger's orders to falsify documents, though he added that he felt indebted to him for helping so many Jews "escape the utter hell of the German Reich." Not surprisingly, Dreifuss was not summoned to testify at Grüninger's trial by Willi Hartmann, the court-appointed defense attorney assigned to the case—and a member of the openly anti-Semitic, ultraconservative Swiss Patriotic Federation—nor were any of the refugees that the two of them collaborated to save.

So Paul Grüninger went down alone, defended by nobody, the ripple effects of his "underhanded practices" contained to himself and his family. At the time her father lost his job, Ruth Rudoner was in Lausanne, enrolled in business school. After his dismissal she had to drop out, come home, and support her parents, or at least try. "I had difficulty getting a job because of my father—there was this fear of Hitler invading Switzerland and all of Europe, and people thought they should not hire someone whose father had been helping the Jews," she told me. "My friends at school—they didn't ask what was happening to me or to my parents, they were all pretty distant."

In the decades that followed, the authorities in St. Gallen conveniently forgot about the Grüninger affair—or rather, remembered just enough to make sure that efforts to revisit it were swiftly rebuffed. The day after I had coffee in Heerbrugg with Ruth Rudoner, I paid a visit to a member of the Swiss Parliament named Paul Rechsteiner, a trim, sprightly man with a mop of shaggy brown hair and a slightly frenetic air. "I'm every time in a hurry," he said with a quick smile as we sat down in his office, which was dominated by books and papers stacked in towering heaps on his desk, a filing cabinet, and broad swatches of the floor. In the mid-1980s, when he was serving as a deputy in St. Gallen, Rechsteiner had locked horns with conservatives who sought to ban a play by the Swiss dramatist Thomas Hürlimann, which was set in World War II and raised pointed questions about attitudes toward Jews. Always in a hurry, Rechsteiner decided to slow down and reexamine his country's past, figuring there was a reason the play had touched a nerve. He soon took a particular interest in Grüninger's case. More than a decade had passed since the disgraced police captain's death. Yet when Rechsteiner introduced a motion to rehabilitate him, he encountered a wave of opposition. "The authorities in the government fought against it, the majority of parties on the right were against it," Rechsteiner told me. "It had something to do with guilt and a period in the history of Switzerland where the attitudes of authority, the attitudes of the state, had such an impact on lives."

Even Ruth Rudoner responded tepidly to his idea, Rechsteiner said, which is understandable. In 1968, when hundreds of fugitives from the Eastern bloc were welcomed into Switzerland after the Soviet Union crushed the Prague Spring, a Swiss politician named Willi Rohner published an article, "Thirty Years Afterward," suggesting that the time had come to reexamine the case of the man who'd been punished for welcoming an earlier wave of refugees fleeing tyranny. "It would be an honor for the canton of Saint-Gallen and for the entire country to correct the mistakes it had made about a man who had ignored inhumane directives at a time when Europe was sinking into barbarism," Rohner wrote. The State Council responded by indicating that, actually, it would not be such an honor. A year later, Ruth Rudoner asked to speak to the council about her father's case; her appeal went nowhere, with one state councilor telling her he'd examined the files and discovered that her father had gotten "rich" the year before he was dismissed.

The effort to bury the past was not entirely successful: Willi Rohner's article was translated into English and came to the attention of some Jewish veterans associations, leading, eventually, to Grüninger's recognition by Yad Vashem. In 1970, the State Council even sent him a letter recognizing his "humane actions." But it ruled out the possibility of reexamining his case. In all, five petitions were introduced to rehabilitate Grüninger, all of them denied. Each time, the old rumors were trotted out, notwithstanding the fact that the main players in the Grüninger affair had long since retired or passed away. Why couldn't state officials simply admit their predecessors had been wrong? Because, of course, it wasn't just the reputation of their predecessors that was at stake: to rehabilitate the man who'd said no to the authorities in Bern in 1938 would have been to issue a searing indictment of the tolerant, neutral country that had condemned him to humiliation and disgrace. Realizing this, a group called Justice for Paul Grüninger decided to commission a historian to probe the veracity of the rumors once and for all. Paul Rechsteiner was a member of the group. When the first scholar approached declined, its members turned to Stefan Keller, perhaps unaware he wasn't so certain they'd be thrilled with the findings he unearthed.

Those findings initially appeared in a series of articles in *Die Wochenzeitung*, a Swiss weekly, and caused a stir, thanks partly to the timing. With the fiftieth anniversary of Normandy approaching and Switzerland's conduct during World War II beginning to fall under critical scrutiny, articles about Grüninger soon surfaced in everything from *The Wall Street Journal* to *Le Monde*. Keller's book became a bestseller in Switzerland. It also spawned a film, by the Swiss director Richard Dindo, much of it shot inside the same wood-paneled courtroom where Grüninger was convicted. In the documentary the trial is reenacted, with some witnesses on hand who weren't invited to appear at the original proceedings—the people Grüninger saved.

One afternoon, at a table by the window of a café in St. Gallen, I met one of these witnesses, a distinguished-looking elderly man with thick dark eyebrows and a shock of wavy gray hair that framed a still-handsome face. He was originally from Vienna, the city he'd fled at age fourteen after witnessing the events of Kristallnacht, following the trail of his brother Herbert. The gray-haired man was Erich Billig. Nearly seventy years had passed since he'd taken flight from Austria. I asked him what he remembered of the experience. "Everything," he said, and, leaning forward slightly, in a tone by turns grateful and bemused, told me the improbable story, pausing only to laugh at his good fortune or to search for the right words in English, which he spoke fairly well, having spent several years working in America at one point. When he got to the part about meeting Paul Grüninger, he recalled the one aspect of his physical appearance that stood out. "He had something I had never seen before—at the end of the glasses there were two chains brought behind the ears," he said. A deep smile creased his face.

After a conversation of no more than ten minutes, Billig told me that Grüninger sent him to the refugee camp in Diepoldsau, and then, having determined it was an inappropriate place for a boy his age, to a Swiss family that sheltered him during the war. Billig got along well with the family, especially with one of the daughters, who later became his wife. They raised three children together. Roughly twenty-five thousand Jews were denied entry into Switzerland during the course of World War II; countless others didn't bother trying. I asked Billig if, after the war, he ever got in touch with Grüninger to express his appreciation, perhaps bringing his kids along to show him how well things had turned out. He shook his head. "Sometimes I thought I should go and see him and say, 'Thank you very much—this is my family thanks to you,'" he said. "But it was really—I hesitated. I had a bad conscience to say 'Now I'm happy and you have problems.' I knew he had problems—it was in the newspapers, not a lot but I read about it." His eyes fell. "I did not have the courage to go."

Before we rose to leave, Billig promised to send me some documents he'd collected about various members of his family. Some time later, I received a yellow envelope in the mail with a cover note dated November 9/10, 2008—Billig had composed it on the seventieth anniversary of Kristallnacht. The first document in the packet was a photocopy of a passport—"Nr. 5396/39"—issued by the German consulate to Erich Ismael Billig in 1938. Emblazoned on it was a swastika and, next to this, the letter *J*, along with a black-and-white photo of a slightly bewildered-looking dark-haired boy. Also in the packet were various maps: an aerial view of the Swiss-Austrian border; a sketch of Europe marked with various places where Billig's relatives had passed through or ended up— Dachau, Buchenwald, Theresienstadt. One other piece of family memorabilia was included, a copy of a letter dated August 31, 1942. It had been sent from Cannes to St. Gallen by Billig's mother, who had stayed in Vienna after sending her sons to Switzerland because she couldn't bear to leave without her husband, who was stranded in Dachau. She eventually left Austria for France and, by August 1942, was in transit to an unknown destination. "My Dearest Erich!" began her letter, which was written in a large, looping script,

Before I leave I send you the dearest kisses from my heart and I wish you all the best and may dear God continue to protect you. Many tender kisses from your mother, who is always thinking of you and hugs you in spirit . . . Temporarily, they put us in the Camp Rivesaltes, and where we will continue from there I do not know yet.

The mystery of where she was heading was cleared up by another document in the packet, indicating that Billig's mother was among the Jews in Deportation no. 29, to Auschwitz. The letter in the looping script was the last thing he heard from her.

After Stefan Keller's book appeared, some of the refugees who had never thanked Grüninger in person got a small chance to make amends, traveling to St. Gallen to attend a meeting with some politicians who'd opposed rehabilitating him in the past. Their presence evidently made a strong impact. "This was very, very impressive," Keller, who arranged the meeting, recalled, "because they couldn't—it was similar to the Grüninger case. If you have the people before you at the same table, the abstraction becomes difficult to deny." Difficult enough that in 1993, forty-five years after his dismissal, the Federal Department of Justice and Police—the division once headed by Heinrich Rothmund—issued a statement expressing "gratitude and respect" to Paul Grüninger and granting the "political rehabilitation long solicited." In 1995, a district court in St. Gallen exonerated Grüninger for "criminal fraud for having backdated records and falsified papers in order to save people's lives."

Thirteen years later, on a damp, drizzly fall morning, a ceremony was held in a small cemetery in Au, a town nestled in a valley surrounded by mountains that were wreathed in heavy mist. Next to the vine-covered wall bordering the final row of headstones, beneath a rain-soaked apple tree, about a dozen people gathered by the grave of Paul and Alice Grüninger. Inscribed on a plaque at the foot of their grave was a now-uncontroversial statement:

PAUL GRÜNINGER

RETTETE

1938/39

VIELE HUNDERT

FLÜCHTLINGE

"Paul Grüninger saved hundreds of refugees in 1938/39." Among the spectators squinting through the rain as a photographer snapped pictures was Paul Rechsteiner. Ruth Rudoner was also there, dressed in a red blouse beneath a black-and-white wool sweater, flanked on one side by Erich Billig, who'd come to pay his respects, and on the other by a middle-aged man in a gray jacket and striped tie— the mayor of Au.

Sixty years after the fact, associating with Paul Grüninger had finally become politically correct. Along with the tree planted for him at Yad Vashem, a courtyard and a football stadium had been named after Grüninger in St. Gallen. A public square in Israel also bore his name. The honors were richly deserved, though they arguably replaced one comforting misrepresentation with another, equally comforting one: the formerly vilified police captain now recast as a hero who did something only a person of exceptional merit could have done.

When asked to explain why he disobeyed the law, Grüninger struck a humbler note, insisting he was simply doing his "human duty." The phrase may reek of false modesty to people whose image of defiance during World War II has been shaped by films such as Jean-Pierre Melville's *Army of Shadows*, a spellbinding portrait of the French Resistance in which a small band of heroic operatives battle the Gestapo while dodging the bullets aimed at their heads. Melville's film presents resistance the way we are accustomed to seeing it: as something that demands superhuman courage, washed in the mythical light of a doomed yet noble cause. But while there were such resisters during World War II, there were others like Grüninger, unexceptional people who took great risks not because they felt drawn to lofty causes but because they were in a position to help someone and did. And then did it again, and again, and again, until what would have seemed unthinkable before came to seem routine, no less routine than enforcing the law became to his peers. As both Hannah Arendt and Stanley Milgram recognized, one reason ordinary people were capable of carrying out unjust orders was habituation: you pulled one switch on the voltage generator, then a couple more, and after a while you stopped agonizing about it, not least since you'd already dirtied your hands a bit.

As counterintuitive as it may seem, might a similar process unfold among people who resist? So contend the psychologists Andre Modigliani and François Rochat. Resistance to authority, they argue, often begins not with grand gestures carried out in the name of abstract causes but "small, modest actions" that rarely seem unusual to the people carrying them out. This is particularly true if the noncompliance starts early, before any compromises are made, as was the case with Grüninger, whose first act of dissent came at the 1938 immigration conference in Bern, where he uncharacteristically rose to express his views, telling his peers it was "impossible" to send the refugees back because the situation on the border was "heartbreaking."

If evil is banal, than surely good must be extraordinary. Rochat and Modigliani argue otherwise, noting the lack of outstanding qualities among the vast majority of Holocaust rescuers who risked their lives to help Jews and how often they spoke less of their heroic conduct than the disjointed world in which they found themselves, an upside-down universe where acting "normal" would have required violating everything they believed. "It is obvious that the attitude I took could not fail to cause strangeness," wrote the Portuguese diplomat Aristides de Sousa Mendes of his irreverent conduct. "However, it should be noted that everything was strange at the time. My attitude was, in fact, a result of the totally abnormal and insuperable circumstances." We honor people like Mendes to redeem them from the mistreatment they endured, but in the process risk diminishing the power of their example, Rochat contends: "Rescuers were very few . . . so that one is tempted to think that they were indeed outstanding people, some kind of saints, or heroes of goodness, which in turn means . . . that they are not like us." In this way, "we keep them away from us, for they are great people, outstandingly good, which we don't think we are."

To claim Paul Grüninger's conduct was the norm would be preposterous. Yet it is equally difficult not to see something unremarkable about him. The former schoolteacher from Au met with refugees, he listened to them, he saw the fear and desperation in their eyes, and so he devised ways to let them stay. His job was to protect people from harm and, guided by nothing more than a capacity to see the refugees as people and a belief that he was honoring his country's founding principles by treating them humanely, this is what he did. The fact that he was not a figure of pristine virtue who seemed destined for heroic things does not detract from the magnitude of his achievement. It makes it more poignant—and, as a commentary on the spirit of his times, more damning.

Paul Grüninger never got to say what he thought of being turned into a hero, but he did get a final opportunity to defend himself, in 1971, when Swiss national television recorded an hour-long program about his case. Before the video was broadcast, the government of St. Gallen threatened legal action if it was depicted unfairly, but the program aired. In one scene, Grüninger is shown standing near the railing on a small bridge at the Swiss-Austrian border. He is dressed in a black top hat, a white shirt, a dark overcoat and tie, peering over the railing at the leafless trees lining the banks of *le vieux Rhin*, which are covered in a thick blanket of pearly white snow. The winter light is pale and bright, and Grüninger blinks repeatedly while gazing at the serene, glistening landscape. He does not smile. He does not speak. His expression is somber but composed. After a while, he ambles across the bridge in a slow, even gait, maintaining his balance with a wooden cane clutched in his gloved right hand. His head is bowed slightly down and, as he shuffles forward, his mouth sags into a pronounced, unmistakable frown. Ruth Rudoner insisted her father was never burdened by resentment after his dismissal, continuing to sing in a choir into his seventies, refraining from voicing complaints. Others who knew him before and after his fall said he became less approachable. An acquaintance named Bernhard Mehl was haunted by "the sad look on his face." This is the look he wears as he crosses the bridge, alone with his memories and, perhaps, his grievances and second thoughts. Has coming to the place that once roused his sympathy jarred loose some bottled-up anger? Might it have stirred a small, uncomfortable pang of regret?

In another scene, Grüninger sits down to field a series of questions. His hat and jacket are off, and sunlight angles through the window onto his cheeks and brow. In his days as a police captain, his full face had lent him a boyish aspect. Now his fleshy jowls accentuate his age. His eyes are heavy and lidded, and the pince-nez he wore has given way to a pair of thick-framed browline glasses perched on the bridge of his nose. "You were aware of the fact that you violated the strict orders of the Swiss government?" he is asked. "Yes, I was certainly aware of that," he says. "But my conscience told me that I could not and may not send them back. And also my human sense of duty demanded that I keep them here." He is asked about the rumors, and tenses up. "Well, I never took a cent," he says, his right eyebrow twitching slightly, the pace of his words quickening. "These people had no money either. They also were the poorest, those that came, and as to how people think, there, I can't change a thing. Many things are said and many lies are told."

The camera continues rolling. One more question is posed. "Would you act in the same way if the situation were the same?"

"Yes, of course," he says without hesitation. "I would do and act exactly the same."

Paul Grüninger was laid to rest one year after this interview was recorded, at a funeral where the choir sang "Nearer My God to Thee" and the Swiss flag was raised. During the ceremony, Rabbi Lothar Rothschild recited a famous passage from the Talmud: "He who saves a single life, saves the entire world."

2. DEFYING THE GROUP

In November 1991, a convoy of buses snaked its way toward Stajićevo, a small village in northern Serbia, carrying several hundred prisoners of war. The buses had come from Vukovar, a town in neighboring Croatia on the banks of the Danube River where, for several months, a fierce battle had raged between Croats and Serbs. In this bloody ethnic skirmish, the Croats had the superior motivation: they were fighting for independence, having voted to secede from Yugoslavia in May. But the Serbs had the superior arms, laying siege to Vukovar from the surrounding hilltops with ordnance supplied by the Yugoslav National Army, which was controlled by the leader of Serbia, Slobodan Milošević. The Serbs struck churches, water towers, factories, monasteries, and beautiful old castles, and eventually the town fell into their hands—what was left of it, that is. Nearly ninety days of indiscriminate bombing turned an enchanting river port into a cratered moonscape of pulverized buildings and spent artillery shells. Rubble was piled thick and high on the roads. Plastic sheets were stretched over the bullet-riddled corpses of the unburied dead.

Soon after Vukovar fell to the Serbs, the men in the town were rounded up, packed onto buses, and driven across the border into

Serbia, to a string of hastily assembled (and conveniently secluded) detention facilities. Among the largest was an abandoned cowshed in Stajićevo. Before filing inside, some of the captives were ordered to pass through a gauntlet of Serbian soldiers, who whacked them with clubs and truncheons as they dashed by. A Croat named Zoran Sangut watched a friend of his get beaten to death before his eyes. He absorbed plenty of harsh beatings himself. Not a lot of mercy was shown, though one restraining factor did exert itself, at least for a while. Before it fell under siege, Vukovar had been home to an assortment of ethnic groups, including tens of thousands of Serbs. Many had fled the town that spring, but not all had managed to leave before the outbreak of hostilities made doing so too dangerous, which meant that mixed in among the prisoners inside the cowshed were some people the soldiers wished to spare from mistreatment: their fellow Serbs. Croats and Serbs speak virtually the same language. They also look a lot alike. Because of this, sifting out their brethren required a degree of knowledge that the Serbs meting out the punishment—who were not from Vukovar—lacked.

This dilemma was resolved, or appeared to be, when one of the officers spotted a familiar face among the prisoners, a big, bearlike man with a large domed head. His name was Aleksander Jevtić, and he was a Serb. Years earlier, Jevtić and the officer had served together in the Yugoslav National Army. The two men exchanged warm greetings. The officer then entrusted Jevtić with a delicate and urgent task, the job of identifying the other Serbs so they could be taken to a separate room.

"Pick carefully," the officer said.

Jevtić nodded and began wading through the knot of prisoners jammed inside the cowshed, who were ranged across a bare cement floor. Some of the men sat slumped and shivering from the cold. Others quietly nursed their wounds, hoping to avoid drawing attention to themselves, since every so often a guard pointed to someone who would then be taken outside for questioning—and, it was understood, more abuse. Not until representatives from the International Red Cross arrived several weeks later to catalogue the prisoners' names would the atmosphere of terror lift. By then, many inmates had been tortured; an unknown number were killed. In the meantime, the task of separating the privileged from the damned fell to Jevtić, who started pointing to various Serbs he recognized. He began kicking at the feet of others, calling out their names and signaling for them to rise. "Come with me, Kovacević," he told one detainee, a trim, muscular man with pale blue eyes who had his head angled down and his hands in cuffs. The man peered up warily but didn't move, because his name wasn't Kovacević, it was Stanko, and he was a Croat, not a Serb.

"Come with me," Jevtić repeated.

Hesitantly, the bewildered man rose to his feet as the Croatian prisoners around him exchanged puzzled glances, wondering what was going on. Jevtić called another Croat forward, and then another, and one more, addressing each by a traditional Serbian name, until prisoners who caught on to what was happening began motioning for him to choose them as well. "Please, please, bring me," they began to whisper.

"Okay, come, hurry," Jevtić replied after peering over his shoulder to make sure none of the guards had overheard.

It went on this way for some time. Jevtić stopped only when no more bodies could be squeezed into the area designated for "Serbs."

Ethnic cleansing, mass violence, pillage, murder, ransacking, rape: so it went in the Balkans in the early 1990s. Neighbors looted the houses of neighbors; friends killed friends. Serbs drove tens of thousands of Croats out of Eastern Slavonia, the region of flat, fertile farmland surrounding Vukovar that they captured (along with the town itself) in 1991. Croats later returned the favor by driving tens of thousands of Serbs out of territory they won back. Both groups inflicted savage violence on Muslims in Bosnia and Herzegovina, where the worst atrocities of the Balkan wars took place, including the massacre of an estimated eight thousand men and boys by Serbian militia in Srebrenica, a crime the International Court of Justice would later deem an act of genocide. Unlike among the diplomats and border guards in countries such as Switzerland during World War II, the binding agent that facilitated much of this conduct was not fealty to the law, and certainly not to any law that carried a presumption of legitimacy: much of the violence that erupted in the Balkans took place in a lawless zone. The binding agent was community, the sense of fellowship that led people with a shared history and common bloodlines to fight—and kill—their former coworkers and acquaintances simply because they belonged to a different ethnic group. Obedience played a role in propelling some of this behavior, but far more important were the effects of conformity and peer pressure: you didn't need explicit orders or even the presence of an authority figure to spur the killing once enough people had internalized the same ideas, assumptions, and fears.

Those who read about the destruction of Yugoslavia from the comfort of a café in Brussels or Brooklyn were likely to feel, in addition to revulsion, a sense of bewilderment and perhaps moral superiority. How could people do such things? How could they succumb so easily to group pressure? And how could so few speak out and resist? Paul Grüninger had had to violate an explicit policy to let refugees into Switzerland during World War II—to betray his superiors, breach an obligation, risk his career. All a Serb theoretically had to do was decide that killing people based on an accident of birth was wrong. What was so difficult about this? Yet Americans need only recall the mood in the United States after September 11, 2001, to appreciate how difficult fear and the specter of a common enemy can make it to speak out against one's community. The fear was far more visceral in the former Yugoslavia, a country with no democratic tradition where identity suddenly became the only ticket to belonging and where crossing the lines of ethnic division could cost you something far more precious than your career.

"Put your mind in that time," a Croat from Vukovar named Predrag Matić told me over coffee one day. An earnest, mild-mannered man who went by the Americanized name Fred, he'd fought on the Croatian side in the war that divided his city and then wound up in Stajićevo, sprawled out on the floor among the other Croatian detainees until Aleksander Jevtić pretended he was a Serb. Fred had grown up in the same neighborhood as Jevtić; they knew each other by first name. Even so, Fred was stunned by what Jevtić did, not least because he understood how quickly his wily ruse could have been exposed and how unforgiving the consequences would have been. "There is no Serb called Ante, there is no Serb called Ure or Stipe," Fred told me. "So in one moment, the officer can say, 'Okay, what's your name?' And you say, 'Ante Zagro.' What can happen to Aleksander Jevtić in that moment?"

What Fred remembered about the cowshed in Stajićevo was being asked how many Serbian children he'd killed and how many Serbian eyeballs he'd gouged out and, when he denied doing these things, being beaten. The guards did not call him a Croat. They called him an "Ustasha," the term for Croatian fascists who'd murdered and persecuted hundreds of thousands of Serbs during World War II. Fred recalled seeing prisoners get dragged outside for questioning and never coming back. He described a Serbian soldier he recognized as an old friend come to his side, crouch down, peel off his glove, and slap him in the face. As he recounted this incident, Fred's cheeks reddened slightly, as though he were reexperiencing the snub. Generally, though, he spoke calmly and dispassionately, in a tone of measured fatalism—this was war, after all—until the subject turned to Aleksander Jevtić and a trace of incredulity entered his voice, as though he still wasn't sure whether what he'd witnessed had actually taken place.

"Now, maybe"—a Serb might help a Croat—"but in that place?

After three months of terrible, terrible, brutal war?" Fred shook his head in disbelief.

As was clear from Fred's description, some of the Serbs in Stajićevo had fun beating up the detainees, extracting added pleasure from humiliating Croats they knew or recognized. But the truth is that you didn't need to enjoy it in order to go along with it. You merely had to be a little weak, or a little passive, or sensitive enough to the shifting weather currents to realize that, as the Croatian writer Slavenka Drakulić observed in her evocative essay "Overcome by Nationhood," which originally appeared in January 1992, the alternative to embracing ethnic nationalism in a region awash in tribal hatred was to stand alone, with no community to call your own. Drakulić likened the experience to slipping on an ill-fitting shirt when staring into an otherwise empty closet: "You may feel the sleeves are too short, the collar too tight. You might not like the color, and the cloth might itch. But there is no escape; there is nothing else to wear. One doesn't have to succumb voluntarily to this ideology of the nation—one is sucked into it."

I. Fears of the Imagination

The outliers who avoided getting "sucked into it" needed to have a vast amount of courage, it went without saying, and they also needed to possess fiercely independent minds, since resisting the wave of ethnic hatred that swept across the Balkans in the early 1990s required performing a dangerous and unpopular act of imaginative resistance. When the journalist Misha Glenny traveled through Serbia and Croatia on the eve of the war, what struck him most was "the homogenization of consciousness" that had taken root. "Croats and Serbs argued endlessly with me as to why Serbs and Croats, respectively, were congenital monsters," wrote Glenny. "They would cite history, religion, education and biology as reasons." Everyone was sure the enemy had it in for them—which, of course, made their own mistrust and hostility seem logical and justified. Nationalism, Glenny concluded, "appears to neutralize that part of the mind which is able to fathom complex equations. Instead, action is motivated by a single Leninist principle: 'Those who are not for us, are against us.'" Aleksander Jevtić had somehow avoided internalizing this us-versus-them thinking, which I assumed had something to do with his education and intellect, a rare skepticism and levelheadedness that enabled him to see past the blinding passions and compellingly simple ideas that drove the logic of hate.

So I imagined while waiting for Jevtić at a train station near Vukovar one day, where we'd arranged to meet. The train I'd told him I'd be taking arrived on time, but there was nobody there. Half an hour passed. Then a black BMW X5 screeched to a halt in front of the station and honked. The window rolled down. "Sorry," said the large, burly man behind the wheel, smiling to reveal a mouth full of yellow teeth, "small problem with police." The sober intellectual I'd envisioned was wearing a white Reebok T-shirt, tan shorts, and shades. His neck and chin were covered in dark stubble, his head was shaved, and his broad face was speckled with moles. He had the girth and heft of a bouncer and, apparently, a ticket somewhere in his sleek new car. He was late because he'd been caught speeding on the way to the station, he told me as I climbed inside.

We zoomed off toward Vukovar, careening along in no apparent fear of being pulled over again. As I would come to learn, Aleksander Jevtić liked driving fast. He also liked sleeping late, hanging out with his friends, and watching sports. When I visited his apartment later, I found him parked in front of a giant flatscreen television in the living room. The books I'd envisioned lining the walls were nowhere to be found. Jevtić, who went by the nickname "Aco" (pronounced "ah-cho"), short for Aleksander, didn't have much patience for reading and possessed no college degree. He hadn't even finished high school. His parents had worked in a shoe factory. On the way to Vukovar, we chatted about tennis, a game at which his eleven-year-old son, Ognjen, one of the top-ranked players in Croatia his age, excelled. "My son, he loves [Rafael] Nadal," said Aco, referring to the Spanish superstar who had just won the French Open and was challenging Roger Federer for the top ranking in the world. Had he once been a distinguished player himself? I asked. "No, no, no!" said Aco with a bellowing laugh, slapping at his ample gut to signal the limits of his appreciation for the game. Chasing down drop shots in the sweltering heat was not his idea of fun, he said. Watching his son practice or Nadal duel against Federer from the comfort of his air-conditioned living room was.

Aco was easygoing and laid-back, to the point of seeming, well, indolent. "I'm lazy," he said after we arrived in Vukovar and made our way into a small room on the ground floor of my hotel to talk. This confession came after I asked Aco how he earned a living, which was apparently by renting out units in a building he'd bought in Novi Sad, a town in Serbia, and converted into several apartments. "I'm not doing anything, just collecting the rent at the beginning of each month," Aco said, swirling the ice in the glass of Coke he'd poured himself. He cracked a sly smile and drained the Coke.

The principled man who'd stunned the likes of Fred Matić in Stajićevo had grown up happily in a country not known for tolerating much dissent. Born in 1966, Aco was reared in the Yugoslavia of Josip Broz Tito, who fashioned a comparatively open brand of communism but, even so, monopolized political power and did not hesitate to toss his few outspoken critics in jail. Aco's parents were not among them. "My mother and my father were Communists," Aco told me. "We had a good life under communism. Perhaps there were problems under communism that I couldn't understand then as a small child." Aco portrayed life in Vukovar during the course of his upbringing as idyllic, particularly when it came to relations between people of different backgrounds. The official motto of

Tito's Yugoslavia was "Brotherhood and Unity," which, later on, when the killing began, would come to seem like a hollow slogan that had been imposed by the regime to cover over and suppress the ethnic tensions simmering beneath the surface. To Aco, the slogan was a faithful reflection of the truth. Nobody bothered to ask a person's ethnicity back then, he said. The shoe factory where his parents worked was Vukovar's largest employer, with a labor force of twenty thousand that reflected the region's diversity—Hungarians, Macedonians, Croats, Serbs; Aco insisted relations were harmonious, with everyone intermingling easily.

The harmony ended in the spring of 1991, when a nationalist government led by Franjo Tudjman was elected in Croatia, to the dismay of many Serbs, who made up 12 percent of the republic's population and who watched with alarm as their Croatian neighbors started draping flags over their balconies emblazoned with the red-and-white-checkered shield known as the *šahovnica*. This was the coat of arms the Ustasha had used back in World War II, when Serbs were being persecuted and killed in massive numbers by an independent Croatian state that was openly aligned with Nazi Germany. Not surprisingly, few such flags were suspended from the terraces of Croatia's Serbs, who instead set about arming themselves, a step encouraged and facilitated by the ruler who'd seized power in Serbia, a former Communist Party apparatchik named Slobodan Milošević. Milošević had other plans for the Serb-populated regions of Croatia, which he dreamed of incorporating into a "Greater Serbia" under his control. Having already abolished the autonomy of two of Yugoslavia's other republics, Kosovo and Montenegro, the Serbian autocrat duly arranged for weapons to be funneled to Serbs in places like the Krajina, an area of Croatia where Serb nationalists formed a separate state, and Eastern Slavonia, where the tensions rose and eventually boiled over. On May 1, a workers' holiday, Croatian police officers entered a Serbian village called Borovo Selo to set some flags adorned with the *šahovnica* on display. Gunfire erupted, and two of the Croats were taken prisoner. The next day, a contingent of Croatian officers set off to rescue them, driving into an ambush that left twelve Croats and five Serbs dead.

Borovo Selo is just north of Vukovar; Aco remembered this incident well. "The war started in Borovo Selo," he told me. From that point forward, it was clear to him "that the situation would become bad." But just how bad evidently wasn't so clear. "I still thought that the situation would calm down," he said. "If I thought it would be a war I would have left, but I thought it wouldn't and I stayed." Aco had relatives in Serbia who had been urging him to get out of Croatia. By the time he decided to flee town, it was too late: the shelling of Vukovar had begun, and all the roads were blocked. With no safe way out, he reluctantly settled on what seemed like the next best option: holing up in an apartment with his girl-friend, Wendy, until the violence died down.

For the next five months, from June to November 1991, Aco focused his attention on a narrow objective: survival. "Three thousand grenades were fired at Vukovar every day," he told me. "Everyone was hiding." He and Wendy avoided setting foot outside. They slept on the floor of the apartment they shared to avoid sniper fire, watching the walls rattle to the incessant thud of the artillery and mortar rounds. Nobody in Vukovar was safe, but the dangers were particularly acute for Serbs, who were now trapped behind enemy lines in a town teeming with Croatian militia locked in a deadly conflict with Milošević's forces. What if word spread that a Serb of fighting age was hiding in their midst? Aco hoped he wouldn't have to find out. "In principle, I wasn't afraid of anything," he told me, "but if someone's best friend gets killed by a Serbian grenade and he finds a Serbian guy"—he pointed his right index finger at his temple and squeezed the imaginary trigger with his thumb—"I would be in big trouble."

Aco, then, understood perfectly well that by 1991 the spirit of "Brotherhood and Unity" had given way to a new reality where the crime of belonging to the wrong ethnic group could get you killed. In truth, as observers fond of pointing to historical precedents never seemed to tire of noting, this reality was not new to many people in the Balkans, something it turned out Aco had learned years earlier, during his childhood.

"Do you know what is Jasenovac?" he asked me at one point in our conversation at my hotel.

"No," I said. "Tell me."

"Jasenovac was a concentration camp during the Second World War, big Ustasha concentration camp," he said. "My mother was in Jasenovac as a child."

"She survived," he said. But the two most important people in her life—Aco's maternal grandparents—did not. "Her parents were killed in this camp," Aco said. "My mother was raised by her aunt. Two years after the Second World War, in 1947, my mother came to Borovo as a war orphan. She went to school there and found my father and married him."

As Aco spoke, it occurred to me that, in fact, I had heard of Jasenovac, or rather read about it, in the book *Blood and Belonging*, a study of nationalism by Michael Ignatieff. Located near the banks of the Sava River, Jasenovac was a massive concentration camp operated with infamous brutality by Croatian fascists during World War II, in the short-lived Independent State of Croatia, which existed between 1941 and 1945. In one scene in the book, which I consulted again shortly after Aco told me this story, Ignatieff visited the grounds, wading through a mountain of shattered glass and shredded debris at a museum and memorial site that had been ransacked. Torn-up photographs of Croatian prelates shaking hands with SS officers, ripped-up prisoners' files: this was Jasenovac in 1992, vandalized, Ignatieff speculated, by Croatian militia eager to blot out an unflattering chapter in their people's history. According to Serbs, the Ustasha exterminated 700,000 people at the camp during World War II, often dumping their butchered corpses straight into the river. Croats put the death toll far lower, at 40,000. Whatever the figure, the scale of the killing—and the enmity it sowed—was vast. It was places like Jasenovac that led some observers to attribute the destruction of Yugoslavia to so-called ancient ethnic hatreds: the long history of fratricidal violence that erupted every couple of generations and made the country's bloody disintegration unavoidable.

The theory was crude and deterministic, ignoring the fact that, for fifty years, the region's various ethnic groups had managed to coexist peacefully, even if it was under a repressive authoritarian system. But, like many crude theories, it contained a kernel of truth. The memory of past affronts was indeed turned into an immensely potent ideological weapon during the turmoil of the early nineties, with nationalists wasting no opportunity to remind people of the tribulations their ancestors had suffered, as a way to foment ethnic hatred. In the speeches of Serbian politicians, on Serbian news channels, in the flood of books, pamphlets, and petitions that were churned out to help prepare the atmosphere for war, the message ceaselessly drummed home was that Serbs like Aco living in places like Croatia would be condemned to relive the humiliation of their ancestors unless they banded together and fought. Didn't they know what would happen if the Ustasha managed to form an independent Croatian state again? Didn't they remember Jasenovac? Weren't they familiar with the narrative of Serbian suffering and victimization that stretched from World War II all the way back to 1389, the year Prince Lazar was defeated by the Turks in the famous Battle of Kosovo? "Only Unity Saves the Serbs" rang the slogan symbolized by the four Cyrillic S's framing the cross on the Serbian nationalist flag, a rallying cry that resonated powerfully among people who heard about clashes in places like Borovo Selo and thought instantly of 1941 or 1389, and whose parents and grandparents could often relay personal stories to them about the horrors of living under the Ustasha.

Given his family history, why didn't this message strike a chord in Aco and lead him to assume the worst about the Croats in Eastern Slavonia? During his childhood, he told me, when his mother recounted what had happened at Jasenovac to her parents, he did assume the worst about them. But when she told him her story, Aco said his mother stressed something else, which is that most Croats were good people and that it was wrong to hate. Aco admitted that he wasn't terribly receptive to the message at first. "I asked my mother: 'Your father and mother were killed in Jasenovac—Croats did it and you tell me that Croats were good? How is that possible?' My mother told me these people who did that were not Croats. They were animals, not humans. Only animals can kill people, not Croats, Serbs, or Muslims. Only animals can do that, animals have no nation, an animal is an animal."

Eventually, he said, the message sank in.

Aco told me this story after I asked him whether he thought of himself as rebellious. "I'm not defiant," he said. "My behavior has to do with the way in which I was raised"—in particular, he said, with his parents, whom he adored. "They taught me to love people. They taught me to respect others and myself. My father used to tell me every day that others would respect me only if I respected myself. That was his maxim."

In his classic book *The Nature of Prejudice*, the psychologist Gordon Allport linked the formation of malignant stereotypes to the habit of sorting people into clusters and categories, some of them rational, others not. Prejudice "is a product of the fears of the imagination," Allport observed, and once such fears become entrenched in a person's mind they are extremely difficult to dislodge ("It is easier . . . to smash an atom than a prejudice," Allport quipped). Aco's personal background should, in theory, have made him peculiarly susceptible to the fears that colored the way Serbs began to imagine Croats as the fabric of trust in Yugoslavia unraveled in the early nineties. But before this happened, an intervention occurred. Before his refusal to conform came another act of refusal: his mother's decision not to bequeath to her son the aggrieved sense of victimhood her story seemed to warrant, and not to encourage him to judge other people by the labels that had cost her own parents their lives.

The lesson imparted by his mother explained why, unlike many other people with a lot more formal schooling, Aco wanted no part of a war where people would once again be tortured, raped, and killed because of who they were. Still, for all of this, there was a mystery at the heart of his story: the mystery of how an unreflective man with no trace of outward idealism, even one raised on an ethic of tolerance, found the nerve to act on this ethic when so many other people adapted their behavior to the spirit of the times. The fact is that goodwill and tolerance had been fairly easy to come by in the former Yugoslavia: a lot of people grew up in towns where nobody kept track of who was a Croat, Muslim, or Serb. Their ideas and, even more so, their conduct shifted abruptly when the political climate changed. Ethnic nationalism could never have flourished otherwise. Nor could it have flourished if many other people with private misgivings about what was happening kept their feelings to themselves, a reaction that was easy to disparage from a distance, less so closer to the maelstrom of events. While covering the war in Bosnia for *The Washington Post*, the reporter Peter Maass grew appalled that so many Serbs could fall silent as unspeakable atrocities took place. Then Maass found himself outside a café where a Muslim man peacefully sipping coffee attracted the unwanted attention of a Serb. "Get out of here, you filth!" snarled the Serb, smashing a beer bottle into the man's shoulder. He began slugging the Muslim with the muzzle of his rifle; then he undid the weapon's safety catch. Maass and two colleagues with him knew exactly what was coming. They proceeded to do the sensible (if not exactly heroic) thing: they fell silent. As it happens, the Muslim's wife appeared and threw herself on her husband, and miraculously the Serb spared them.

Afterward, Maass concluded that he and his colleagues had acted understandably—the Serb was armed, after all, and they were not. Who knew whether intervening might not have provoked him? "But it didn't feel very good," he wrote. "A man was on the verge of being executed in cold Balkan blood, and we stood aside because it was the prudent thing to do. Was it much different from the Serbs who prudently kept quiet as their Bosnian neighbors were shot or packed off to prison camps?"

What Maass faced—two very bad choices—turned many decent people into passive bystanders, and others into perpetrators. Among the latter was a soldier named Drazen Erdemović, who in July 1995 was ordered to help carry out the massacre of Muslims trapped in the UN "safe area" of Srebrenica. Erdemović refused, he later claimed, and was told that, if this was the case, he'd be shot as well. He didn't want to die, and so he proceeded to kill, shooting dozens of Muslims who were brought by bus to the Branjevo Farm, lined up, and slaughtered in groups of ten. When the last of the victims had fallen, Erdemović was told there were more still on the way; this time he successfully resisted. Erdemović was not among the killers at Srebrenica who shot Muslims with callous glee—he was actually a Croat who'd enlisted in a multiethnic unit he thought would help him avoid combat duty. He later volunteered to testify about the massacre before the International Criminal Tribunal for the former Yugoslavia. This didn't stop the ICTY from holding him accountable for his acts. It did prompt the court to reduce his sentence, in a judgment that concluded his only choice was "to kill or be killed."

II. Moral Sentiments

Why didn't Aco conclude he, too, had no choice but to kill or be killed? Did he simply not register fear the way ordinary people do? Or perhaps did he harbor a subversive streak that lent danger a perverse thrill in his eyes, the same frisson of excitement that shaped his driving habits? Not leaving Vukovar sooner in 1991 had, in fact, struck some of Aco's relatives as reckless. His older sister pleaded with him to pack up his bags earlier—pleas he ignored, he told me, in a pattern that was apparently familiar. "I've never listened to my sister," Aco sighed. "All my life she would say, 'Aco, listen, be careful!'" He rolled his eyes. "She's two years older but behaves like a mom."

But if Aco was less cautious than his sister, he was not a fool: eventually, when it became clear that war was inevitable, he came around to her view. He would have left Vukovar and gone to Serbia if it had been safe enough. His reckless streak did not prevent him from exercising caution during the war, when he kept his presence in Vukovar hidden. And he would have exercised caution in Stajićevo as well, he told me, had a sudden urge not gripped him.

"It was an instinct," he said of his decision to start making up names for the Croatian detainees in the cowshed. "I thought these people needed help the most, from the look in their eyes."

So he just decided to help them, based on the look in their eyes?

"I decided, just like that," he said. "Some [of the prisoners] were wounded, some hurt, and some beaten."

Yet the officer's instructions were clear—that he should pick only Serbs?

"Yes, the officer told me to pay attention to what I did," Aco said. "Soldiers were coming, but the building was long and there were only a few of them.

"Nevertheless," he acknowledged, "I had to be fast."

Aco acted fast, and he apparently acted without thinking too much about the consequences, which, on one level, made sense: stopping to weigh his options almost surely would have given him pause. Still, it was striking—and, to me, strange—that what he described was a reflex, an impulsive reaction, as though all he'd had to do was allow his instincts to guide him, as though all that was necessary was to listen to the feelings in his gut. This struck me as odd because, in college, the philosophers I'd read in courses on the history of Western thought all seemed to agree that moral behavior demanded precisely the opposite: not following base emotions but reining them in to avoid behaving like Hobbesian brutes. "Have courage to use your own reason!" proclaimed Immanuel Kant, articulating the Enlightenment credo that morality had to be grounded in universal, abstract, rational laws. The key to acting ethically was remaining dispassionate, the rationalists of the Enlightenment maintained, which is why I'd come to Vukovar expecting to meet a Kantian type, a cool deliberator who would have scored high on the moral development scale created by Lawrence Kohlberg. Drawing on the work of the Swiss psychologist Jean Piaget, Kohlberg linked ethical advancement to higher-order stages of reasoning. Children at the "pre-conventional" stage of morality responded to dilemmas by thinking solely of their egotistical concerns ("What's in it for me?"); those at the "conventional" level drew on social rules and conventions; and those at the highest, "post-conventional" stage, on universal ethical norms. The mechanism that enabled people to pass from one stage to the next—to think beyond themselves and begin to take account of the rights of others—was not emotional but intellectual. "Affective forces are involved in moral decisions, but affect is neither moral nor immoral," Kohlberg maintained. "The moral channeling mechanisms themselves are cognitive."

The story Aco told about what impelled him to act did not fit easily into this framework. But it did mesh with an alternative view that in recent years has begun to challenge the Kantian paradigm, a theory emphasizing the pivotal role that base emotions play in our moral lives. One proponent of this view is Antonio Damasio, a neuroscientist who some years ago began to treat a patient who'd had a tumor surgically removed from the cortex of his brain, in the area behind the nasal passages. The surgery had not damaged the man's cognitive abilities: his memory was sharp; he scored high on IQ tests; he even performed well on a modified version of the test designed by Lawrence Kohlberg to determine how people resolve ethical dilemmas. Yet the patient had ceased being able to make basic decisions. He began investing his money poorly, ignoring the advice of friends, and flubbing assignments at work. It seemed mystifying that a rational, intelligent person would act in such ways, until it dawned on Damasio that impaired logic might not be the problem. He began to notice that when the patient talked about his life, his tone was weirdly flat. Shown images of houses burning and bloody accidents, he confessed to feeling nothing. The same pattern surfaced in other patients who'd suffered damage to the same part of the brain—smart, reasonable people who seemed oddly detached and who began doing things (investing in shady businesses, mistreating friends) that suggested poor judgment and character. Patients who had suffered the brain lesion early in life were particularly damaged—lying, stealing, and showing an alarming lack of guilt, remorse, or empathy.

What caused this behavior was not a dearth of reason but an inability to generate emotions, scientists studying the inner workings of the brain have come to believe, and it is these emotions that inform our moral judgments and enable us to care about other people. So contends the moral psychologist Joshua Greene, who has illustrated the salience of feelings by asking people to contemplate two scenarios about a runaway trolley that is about to run over five people. In the first scenario, subjects are asked whether it would be okay to press a switch that will divert the trolley to a different track so it will kill only one person. Nearly all say yes. In the second scenario, they are asked whether it would be okay to push a large man onto the track, killing him to save five. Most say no. From a utilitarian perspective, the scenarios are equivalent, but our minds don't process them the same way. When a subject is mulling over the first scenario, Greene has shown, the parts of the brain that are associated with rational decision-making light up on an

MRI scanner. When the subject is contemplating the second scenario, areas related to the emotions are activated. Subjects hesitate because of a natural, perhaps even evolutionary aversion to harming someone directly, and this gives them pause. According to Greene, the dilemma in the first scenario is "impersonal," whereas in the second it is "personal," which makes it far more difficult to stomach. For a moral violation to register as personal "requires that the victim be vividly represented" and that the resulting harm spring "in a vivid way from an agent's will."

Why did Heinrich Rothmund find it easy to sign laws barring refugees from entering Switzerland during World War II while sitting at his desk in Bern, but not when he had to face them directly near the French border, in Boncourt? Not because his reasoning changed, but because, as he later put it, he "did not have the heart to expel them"—because an issue swathed in abstractions became vivid and personal and his logical assumptions gave way to his feelings. The capacity to feel sympathy doesn't necessarily require having sophisticated knowledge or advanced reasoning skills. Some biologists argue it doesn't even require being human. The primatologist Frans de Waal, one of the world's leading authorities on bonobos, has documented displays of compassion performed by these good-natured mammals—our closest cousins in the ape family—not only toward their own offspring but also toward other species, such as injured birds. The idea that reason is needed to tame the passions is closely linked to the notion that, but for this, human beings would behave like animals, doing what came naturally to them. In de Waal's view, this may be true, but what comes naturally to us isn't necessarily so destructive and pernicious. "We are born with impulses that draw us to others and that later in life make us care about them," he argues.

Viewed in this light, the fact that Aco followed "an instinct" rather than being guided by his rational faculties appears less odd.

The reason people think something is right or wrong indeed comes later, some moral psychologists contend: what happens first is an affective intuition. This new "emotivist" view of morality actually has a distinguished pedigree. According to the philosopher David Hume, moral knowledge is grasped through an "immediate feeling and finer internal sense," not a "chain of argument and induction." The emphasis on feelings rather than inductive reasoning was shared by Adam Smith, the British economist famous today for *The Wealth of Nations* but better known during his own life for another book, *The Theory of Moral Sentiments*, which probed the nature of sympathy and "fellow feeling." "How selfish soever man may be supposed, there are evidently some principles in his nature, which interest him in the fortune of others, and render their happiness necessary to him, though he derives nothing from it, except the pleasure of seeing it," wrote Smith. "Of this kind is pity or compassion, the emotion which we feel for the misery of others, when we either see it, or are made to conceive it in a very lively manner."

If the scientists who in recent years have begun to sprinkle their papers with references to Hume and Smith are right, could it be that what impelled Aco to act in the cowshed was less a choice than a reflex—an "immediate feeling" that welled up instantaneously, triggered by the neurons that began firing in the area of the brain responsible for activating pity and compassion? And, to take the thought one step further, that what determines the intensity of such activity is not a person's values or ideas but how their brain happens to be hardwired? A 2009 study published in *Proceedings of the National Academy of Sciences* indeed linked higher levels of empathy to an oxytocin receptor that varies genetically and functions as a neurotransmitter. Subjects with a particular genetic variant scored consistently higher on an empathy test measuring the ability to infer the mental state of others. Could Aco have simply been born with a "sympathetic brain" that made him unusually prone to making such inferences?

It's an alluring idea. It is also a dubious one, not least since, as with Stanley Milgram's study of obedience, there are limits to how much a lab experiment—even one conducted with sophisticated brain-imaging technology—can tell us about how people will act in the real world, as some researchers acknowledge. "An MRI scanner can show us whether blood flow in the brain increases when a subject is shown, say, a picture of a person suffering," says Dilip Jeste, a psychiatrist who has written about the neural correlates of wisdom and empathy. "But whether someone would go and do something for that person is another question. When we say we are measuring empathy, it's a lab condition. Whether it translates into something in real life—we don't know." The brain is not an inert organ, Jeste adds, which is why assessing its qualities is not quite like measuring a person's height or weight. "One of the biggest advances in brain research is the demonstration of neuroplasticity, which means that the brain can change, not just functionally but structurally," he says. "When we say someone is hardwired, we often give too much credit to our genes, but actually the expression of genes is more under our control than we think. The brain is not like steel, it's like plastic, and it is affected by the environment. I don't think you can just look at the gray matter and say, 'Oh, he has twice as much empathy and therefore he will act differently.' It ignores the influence of upbringing, environment, culture."

There is one other reason to avoid drawing sweeping conclusions from studies showing that emotions such as empathy may be "hardwired," something scientists inclined to quote Adam Smith would do well to recall. Unlike David Hume, who portrayed sympathy as an automatic reflex, Smith argued in *The Theory of Moral Sentiments* that the ability to feel pity and compassion involved conscious effort. It was a function of the imagination, an instrument that enabled even the "greatest ruffian" to put himself in the shoes of a person being tortured and identify with his suffering, but that could also be skewed and disabled—by fear, by chauvinistic ideas, by ideological blinders that could quickly turn moral sentiments into immoral ones. "It is by the imagination only that we can form any conception of what are his sensations," wrote Smith of the observer who sympathizes with a torture victim. Smith described this imaginary victim as "our brother." But what if we don't imagine him as a brother? What if we imagine him as an enemy—an "Ustasha," or a piece of Muslim "filth"?

Not long after my first trip to Vukovar, I traveled to Trebinje, a small town nestled in a valley in the Republic of Srpska, twenty minutes from the beautiful coastal city of Dubrovnik, to interview a Serb named Rade Aleksić. We met on the ground floor of a lavender stucco building with pomegranate trim that houses the pizzeria he owns, on a scorching day in mid-July. Tall and bald, with pale eyes and a gently weathered face, Rade sipped a glass of orange juice while telling me a story about his son, Srdjan, a gifted swimmer and amateur actor who, on January 21, 1993, sat with some friends at a café in the town square. Srdjan was not a political person, Rade said, but "he loved this town, he loved the people here," which is why, that day, without explaining the reason to his friends, he rose from the table suddenly. He had spotted someone he knew, a Muslim named Alen Glavovic, getting accosted by a Serbian soldier. The soldier was large and drunk and had forced Glavovic to the ground, pressing a knife to his throat. Srdjan leapt into the fracas and helped the Muslim escape.

It was an impulsive reaction, driven by compassion, but it wouldn't have happened if what Srdjan had felt and imagined at that moment had been shaped by the prevailing mood of bigotry and hate. We know this because, before returning to the café with his friends, Srdjan was confronted by some Serbs whose sympathies were shaped by this mood and who decided to express their feelings in a different way. The men began belting and pummeling Srdjan near the steps of the police station, in broad daylight, with plenty of people standing around. Nobody came to his defense, though a woman who witnessed the mêlée did rush to call Rade.

"Please come, they're killing your son at the marketplace!" she screamed into the phone. By the time Rade arrived, Srdjan had been wheeled into the emergency room of the local hospital, blood-spattered and unconscious. He fell into a coma and, a few days later, was pronounced dead, at the age of twenty-six.

III. Standing Alone

The men who murdered Srdjan Aleksić had stunted moral imaginations, one could argue. But one could also argue they were driven by another base emotion that is hardwired and universal: the desire to feel a sense of belonging. In his arresting account of the 1994 Rwandan genocide, Philip Gourevitch showed that part of what led Hutus to join the campaign to exterminate Tutsis was the sense of camaraderie that banding together against a common enemy generated. Genocide "is an exercise in community building," Gourevitch observed—"it brought people together." One perpetrator likened hunting down Tutsis to "communal work duty," and admitted that he'd enjoyed it. "The genocide was like a festival. At day's end, or any time there was an occasion, we took a cow from the Tutsis, and slaughtered it and grilled it and drank beer . . . It was a festival. We celebrated."

Only backwards people from underdeveloped countries can come together in such ghastly endeavors, the civilized world often likes to tell itself. But the desire for fellowship is universal and has not infrequently been channeled into murderous projects in countries that are materially advanced. "Man has a horror of aloneness. And of all kinds of aloneness, moral aloneness is the most terrible kind." The quotation is from Honoré de Balzac and appears in Erich Fromm's classic study of authoritarianism, *Escape from Freedom*, in which the Frankfurt School psychologist sought to explain why more Germans did not oppose Hitler. Fromm traced the answer not to mindless obedience but to the terror of feeling alienated from one's community and to the tremendous desire to belong. "When other political parties were abolished and the Nazi party was Germany," he observed, "opposition to it meant opposition to Germany. It seems that nothing is more difficult for the average man to bear than the feeling of not being identified with a larger group. However much a German citizen may be opposed to the principles of Nazism, if he has to choose between being alone and feeling that he belongs to Germany, most persons will choose the latter."

What Fromm observed of Germans during World War II was true of most Serbs and Croats in Yugoslavia a half century later, and for that matter of most people in Vukovar long after the fighting had stopped. In 1998, the war-blasted city where Aco grew up had been reincorporated into Croatia, under an agreement overseen by the United Nations, which dispatched thousands of peacekeepers to demilitarize the surrounding region in the hope of preventing violence from flaring up again. With peace would come reconciliation, it was hoped: the rubble would be cleared, displaced Croatian refugees would return (while Serbs who'd settled in the town after the war would remain), and Vukovar would reemerge as the charming multiethnic city it had been.

But while further violence had been averted, no reconciliation had occurred. Physically, Vukovar looked eerily frozen in time, the roads still pitted with holes gouged into the pavement by the mortar shells that had rained down from the surrounding hilltops in 1991, the infrastructure in staggering disrepair. Crumbling buildings like the bullet-pocked concrete pile next to my hotel, once a popular department store, sat caked in dust and abandoned. I peered into it one day and spotted a dead mouse and two dead birds amid shards of broken plaster and rotting garbage. A bit farther down in the opposite direction stood the Vukovar Museum, in a dilapidated two-story building with boarded-up windows and a shrapnel-shredded brick façade. Inside the museum, a skein of cobwebbed wires hung from the ceiling in a cavernous room with bare cement floors and a few randomly mounted paintings on display.

Fire-blackened walls, collapsing roofs, the naked beams of gutted buildings nobody had gotten around to demolishing yet: you could scarcely walk a block in Vukovar without being reminded of the damage wrought by the war. The concentration of blighted buildings and decomposing masonry—a shell-damaged water tower here, a half-wrecked train station there—made it seem that 1991 was only yesterday and that very little forgetting had been done, which was indeed the case. Croats now had their city back, but living among them were thousands of Serbs they believed had blood on their hands. Serbs, in turn, felt like they'd been made into scapegoats for fighting a war that never would have happened if Croats hadn't sought to break up Yugoslavia and form an independent state.

Compounding the rift about the past was resentment born of competition for a shrinking pool of mostly dead-end jobs: the shoe factory that once powered the local economy was now a moldering ruin on the outskirts of the city, and the camaraderie among former coworkers had given way to mutual barbs. The few good opportunities that came around invariably fell to Croats, Serbs would tell you. Serbs were merely nostalgic for the privileges they'd enjoyed in Yugoslavia, Croats would respond. The two groups rarely talked to each other, a Hungarian named Laslo told me one morning as we strolled through town. "Here," he said, pointing at a café with a yellow awning in the main commercial square, "Serbs drink coffee." "Here," he said, motioning at the establishment directly across from it, which had a brown awning, "Croats drink coffee." At both cafés, a handful of patrons sat slumped in their chairs, smoking cigarettes and casting listless glances at the occasional passerby. While their parents took pains not to brush shoulders in coffee shops, Serbian and Croatian children attended school in separate shifts, Laslo said. A Croat named Jacques later explained to me why there was little mixing anymore. "In every corner of this town I know where friends of mine died," he said. "We don't talk to them, and they don't talk to us."

Aco wasn't lumped in with "them" by Croats familiar with his story, one might have imagined, and, on my second visit to Vukovar, I stayed with the family of a man who needed no convincing on this point. His name was Zoran Sangut, the prisoner in Stajićevo who'd watched a friend of his get beaten to death by the guards. At the time, he told me, he thought he'd be killed as well, and he believed this up until the moment he watched in shock as Aleksander Jevtić began kicking at the Croats and directing them to the other room so they would be spared. Zoran, who had a high-pitched laugh and an air of melancholy that offset his otherwise laid-back manner, was among the Croats chosen. He was now a lawyer. He was also a Croatian nationalist deeply committed to the idea that there should be a place in Croatia for all ethnic groups, a view undoubtedly informed by the fact that but for this, he might not have been alive. At a café in Zagreb beforehand, he told me that, years earlier, he'd run into Aleksander Jevtić on the street for the first time since the drama in the cowshed had unfolded. I asked him what he said to him. "Thanks," he told me with the sheepish look of a man who clearly felt he could never repay the debt. "Thanks, thanks, thanks."

Zoran had since struck up a friendship with Aco, and a few years after their chance encounter, he decided to express his gratitude more publicly, in a letter to the president of Croatia, Stjepan Mesić. "With this letter, I plea for a medal to be awarded to Mr. Aleksandar Jevtić for saving between 150–200 lives of Croats who defended the city of Vukovar," he wrote in the petition, which was postmarked November 9, 2005. "Aleksandar Jevtić showed great courage and humanity, risking his own life. Therefore, I plea for an appropriate award for his actions."

Such honors weren't rare in Vukovar: on streets where pivotal battles had occurred, in the town hospital, along the promenade bordering the Danube, plaques and monuments abounded. The town was a veritable shrine to the fallen heroes of 1991—a martyr city that some Croats referred to simply as "Hero Town." Yet three years later, Zoran Sangut had yet to receive a reply to his letter, and the reason wasn't hard to guess. In the official Croatian narrative of the war, Serbs were featured as the villains and Croats as the plucky heroes who'd taken up arms to defend Vukovar against unprovoked aggression. There was little space in this narrative for an exemplary Serb, and, Zoran Sangut aside, not a lot of Croats in Vukovar were clamoring to change this. Many of Aco's Croatian neighbors indeed treated him shabbily precisely because he was a Serb who couldn't be thrust into the role reserved for their ethnic group, I was informed. Fred Matić told me a story illustrating how deep this impulse ran. Every day, he said, Aco drove his son to practice tennis in a facility about forty miles from Vukovar. A few months earlier, Aco heard about an arena in town nobody used during the winter, so he asked around to see if his son could practice there. He was told he had to obtain permission from the man in charge, a Croat who was one of the prisoners he'd picked out in Stajićevo. The man denied Aco's request. "Because he's Serb," said Fred. "They don't say that, but they think it."

Aco felt more at home among Vukovar's Serbs, one might have thought, but here he ran up against the opposite problem: the perception that, ultimately, he wasn't really one of them either, on account of his wayward conduct during the war. "Aleksander has two kinds of problems," explained Fred. "Croats don't like him because he's Serb. Serbs don't like him because they know he helped Croats."

Aco hadn't mentioned any of this during our initial encounter. The next time I saw him was at a café where Zoran Sangut had invited a couple of friends to get together for a drink. We met at the Havana Club, an aquatic-themed establishment with blue-and-white pillows adorned with dolphins and boat anchors propped up on the outdoor benches, which looked out on a dreary cluster of shell-scarred apartment buildings that made the ocean seem very far away. It was nearing dusk, the low sun casting a reddish glow on the ribbon of clouds strung across the sky. Aco showed up at his customary time—half an hour late—dangling his keys in his right hand and in seemingly jolly spirits, as though he, at least, was ready for a cocktail after a leisurely day at the beach. How was life? I asked him. "Good," he said, smiling widely. "Life is bitch!" He greeted Zoran with a friendly shoulder clap and sat down. I told him I didn't mean to dampen his spirits, but that I'd heard a bit about his troubles. I brought up the incident involving the tennis arena. Aco nodded, and made clear I was by no means dampening his spirits. "I don't care," he said flatly, looking me straight in the eye. I said I'd heard he wasn't terribly popular among Serbs either. "No," he acknowledged, grinning, "maybe because I'm not beautiful, like Zoran." He let out a hearty laugh.

"Look, I have friends," he said after he'd stopped chuckling. "Zoran is my friend. You're my friend. You can't please everyone."

Aco clearly didn't try terribly hard to please everyone, something I soon came to appreciate firsthand. After he'd told me his son was a tennis prodigy, I asked whether I could watch him play sometime, maybe even hit a few balls together. Some weeks later, I returned to Vukovar with an invitation to do this. On Saturday morning, around ten o'clock, I dialed Aco's number. It rang and rang, but there was no answer. I tried again half an hour later, and this time, after a dozen or so rings, a man picked up the phone and mumbled a muffled greeting into the receiver. I identified myself and asked for Aco, realizing as I was doing so that I was speaking to him and that I'd woken him up. "Sorry," I muttered meekly, "I'll call you later." "Yes, please," he replied, and then hung up. Oh well, I figured, we'd work out the details later. But I was wrong. Aco put me off the entire weekend. He didn't want to be bothered. Eventually he informed me over the phone that it would be better if I came back another time. "Okay," I said, straining to sound polite while privately fuming. Couldn't he have told me this before I'd made the trip? Didn't he know this wasn't a terribly effective way to make a good impression on a reporter—or an endearing way to treat a "friend"?

What I failed to appreciate was that Aco wasn't in the business of making good impressions. If you liked him, fine. If you didn't, so be it. He wasn't going to lose sleep either way, and he certainly wasn't going to go out of his way to please you. His obliviousness to what others thought wasn't necessarily his most becoming feature. But it had served him well in 1991, reflecting a quality analyzed in another famous behavioral experiment. Its designer was Solomon Asch, a social psychologist who in the 1950s brought volunteers into a classroom and asked them to match a black vertical stripe on a white card with one of three comparison stripes on another card. The lengths of the stripes differed enough that any child could tell them apart. But in the experiment, Asch placed each subject among a group of people who were confederates of his. The confederates sat in rows and were told to announce their choices aloud, with the actual subject seated in back, so that he had to answer after some of his peers did. At a certain point, the confederates started giving wrong answers, which they all agreed on. Would the subject go along?

When Asch collated the results, he found that only one-fourth of the participants were able to get through the eighteen-comparison exercise without yielding to the group at least once. In interviews afterward, subjects gave reasons for capitulating—the fear of being seen as "black sheep," "weak-headed," "queer"—that illustrated the power of what Asch termed "the majority effect." Breaking down the results by educational background, Asch found that a person's level of schooling made little difference in his or her ability to resist this effect. What mattered instead was a willingness to tolerate a certain kind of social discomfort, "the painfulness of standing alone," which was by far the most common reason individuals gave for submitting to the group.

A half century later, a team of researchers at Emory University carried out an updated version of the Asch experiment, this time with subjects asked to determine whether various three-dimensional objects flashing on a computer screen were different or the same. The answer was obvious, but when confederates started making deliberate blunders, the error rate ballooned. The researchers at Emory were also interested in what enabled some people to defy the group, and, using fMRI scanners, they examined the neurological activity that took place when this happened. What they found was that heightened stimulus occurred in the amygdala, two almond-shaped lobes of the brain associated with autonomic arousal—in particular, with fear. According to Gregory Berns, a neuroscientist who helped design the study, "this alone may explain a person's ability not to conform. A lot depends on a person's willingness to tolerate that fear, that pain."

IV. Solidarity

Perhaps, then, it was true: Aco didn't register fear the way many other people did, not the fear of being shot and killed but the fear of being regarded as a black sheep, of "standing alone." Far more than Paul Grüninger, he needed not to care what his peers and fellow citizens thought of him, and as far as I could tell, he didn't. He had the thick skin and individualistic temper of what the sociologist David Riesman would have called an "inner-directed" personality, which may have explained why, despite being a misfit, he didn't seem unhappy. To the contrary, he seemed profoundly, almost eerily, content. The fact he hadn't gotten recognized for his conduct? Aco claimed this didn't bother him. The fact that no more than ten of the men he'd picked out in the cowshed had so much as said thanks? "I'm not asking people to thank me, I'm not bothered by it and I'm not offended." This was not because he lacked pride but because his sense of pride was internally generated. "Everybody's different, but I feel great today," he told me. "Every morning, I look at myself in the mirror and I have a big smile. I'm a happy man."

During the weekend I spent waiting to meet Aco's son, I read a novel called *The Speaking Cure*, by David Homel, about some unhappy men. The novel tells the story of a Serbian psychologist who is assigned to field incoming calls at a mental health clinic established to help soldiers deal with the aftershocks of the war. The callers to the clinic unburden themselves of the nightmares and fixations swirling through their unquiet minds: a soldier who has developed an obsession with counting the exit wounds on corpses; another who wants to track down the woman he raped to profess his love to her. The psychologist comes to see their disturbed and fractured psyches as a mirror of their fractured homeland. "All my patients suffered from some form of trauma born of our civil war," he reflects. "Yet our government would not even tolerate us calling our war civil; the patients were not allowed to name their disease. It tried to forbid us from viewing our former fellow countrymen . . . as anything but aggressors, invaders, illegal occupiers, people without identity, people without pasts or with counterfeit pasts. But it really was civil war, and I encouraged my clients to see it that way. A civil war is nothing if not a long and sustained assault against one's own self."

What the novel suggested—that the people who'd been swept up in the tide of nationalism had ended up doing violence not only to others but also to themselves—came to mind often while I was in Vukovar, including at a bar one night when I struck up a conversation with a Serb named Darko Ivanov. He was forty-one but looked ten years older, a gaunt, fidgety man with a gray pallor who told me his story while drinking beer and chain-smoking Largo cigarettes. In 1991, Darko had fought on the Serbian side in the battle for Vukovar, manning a crest known as German Hill. "I go to war to save this country, I went to war to save Yugoslavia—this was the only reason," he said, blowing a column of smoke through his nose and showing me his black-and-red lighter, which was engraved with an image of Tito. "Yugoslavia, it's here, it's here," he said, tapping the index finger of his right hand on his heart. Twenty days into the fighting, Darko got wounded, from a bullet that grazed his left thigh, but he soon returned to the front lines, to the task of saving his country and, he said, to more wounds. Darko saw the house in which he'd grown up get burned to the ground; he woke up one day to the news that his father-in-law had been killed. Eventually he began to suffer epileptic attacks and seizures. "This was a terrible time," he said. "Twenty-four hours a day. It was a big stress." At the bar, Darko knocked back his beers the same way he lit up his cigarettes—one after another, with brisk, joyless efficiency—and at one point he leaned forward through the haze of smoke, pupils dilated from alcohol, and insisted it had all been necessary because Croats had chosen to destroy Yugoslavia. He said it firmly, and he clearly believed it, but the words had a slightly hollow ring, coming from a man who seemed as damaged by the war as Vukovar seemed, with a wellspring of bitterness that enveloped him as thickly as the smoke. "Yugoslav Army tried to save the same country as me, because I'm Yugoslav," he said, "but politics—politics is whore. Tudjman and Milošević, they eat and drink together.

"War," he said after a few more beers, "war is never a good cause."

Aco lived in a town full of people like Darko and, not surprisingly, he didn't envy them. He had something they lacked—a clean conscience—and nobody could say he hadn't earned his right to the happiness this afforded him. But his indifference to what other people thought, coupled with his conspicuous detachment from current events and politics—topics he waved aside impatiently whenever I brought them up—was hard not to find slightly disconcerting, and underscored what his gesture of defiance in the cowshed was not. There were people in the Balkans who responded to the eruption of ethnic nationalism with acts of civic engagement: attending peace demonstrations, circulating petitions, joining opposition parties. Aco did none of these things. He didn't lift a finger to stop the war from happening; he just tried to sit it out, and then, on the basis of an emotional impulse, to help some people, and then, after this, to go back to enjoying his life. He'd acted nobly, to be sure, and saved many lives, but one could easily imagine the courageous activists who'd organized demonstrations during the war wondering why people like him weren't out on the streets with them. Didn't Yugoslavs opposed to ethnic violence have an obligation to make their voices heard? And didn't Aco crave being connected to some larger purpose or cause?

One could, of course, imagine people like Darko who'd chosen sides in the war asking the same thing. Along with fellowship and security, a larger sense of purpose is what nationalism engenders, lending meaning to the struggles and sacrifices of those who live— and sometimes die—for the cause. One afternoon, Zoran Sangut drove me down a gravelly road hedged by cornfields to a seemingly isolated stretch of farmland. Zoran parked, got out, and led me to a clearing lined with bushes planted in tidy rows on a rectangular lot sprinkled with white pebbles. We were in Ovčara, where, on November 20, 1991, shortly after they'd seized control of Vukovar, Serbs massacred more than 250 civilians and former combatants who'd been rounded up at the hospital, dumping their bodies in a ditch that had since been turned into a memorial site. An old man and a young boy were leaving as we arrived. We exchanged silent nods and then had the place to ourselves, save for the beads, votive candles, and miniature crosses strewn on the markers next to the bushes, one planted for each victim of the massacre. Zoran circled the grounds slowly, his hands tucked in the pockets of his shorts, his face a solemn mask. We followed a path to the edge of a marble monument engraved with the *šahovnica* and, at its base, an enormous wreath of red and white flowers tied up with red, white, and blue ribbons—the colors of the Croatian flag.

Afterward we drove to a nearby cemetery, walking through rows of flower-bedecked tombstones to a sun-blanched field covered in a sea of white crosses. Planted in the ground next to the crosses were hundreds of small Croatian flags that fluttered in the breeze. To our right was a sculpture made of four towering slabs of turquoise stone arranged so that, from all four sides, they framed the air into the shape of a cross. At the base of the monument was a torch and, beneath this, the words "For Soldiers of Vukovar," a dedication that would not have surprised the historian Benedict Anderson. "No more arresting emblems of the modern culture of nationalism exist than cenotaphs and tombs of Unknown Soldiers," observed Anderson in his seminal book *Imagined Communities*, which argued against seeing nationalism as a cousin of political ideologies like fascism (to which its more extreme incarnations were often compared). According to Anderson, the closer analogy was to religion, with similarly deep questions posed— Why had these young men died? What could the living do to honor them?—and similar comfort drawn from the shared belief that some measure of redemption could be extracted from the noble sacrifices of one's forebears.

"I don't like going where dead people are," Aco told me when I asked him later whether he'd ever been to these memorial sites. In the same conversation, I asked him how he identified himself. He paused. Then he said, "I'm a citizen of the world," a phrase whose airy abstractness made me think of the essay Slavenka Drakulić had written back in 1992. It was possible to say no to nationalism, Drakulić had suggested, but at the price of standing naked, with no community to call one's own. Aco didn't mind this because, oddly and somewhat unnervingly, solidarity with other people who shared his values and ideals was not something that mattered to him.

Or so I thought until, one evening, I dropped by his apartment with Zoran Sangut. Greeting us at the door was Aco and a slender, attractive woman with shoulder-length sandy blond hair and a shy smile. Her name was Wendy, the same Wendy who had been Aco's girlfriend back in 1991, and who was now his wife. Barefoot in a black T-shirt and cargo pants, Wendy showed us into a spacious living room with a large burgundy leather couch flanked by matching armchairs, arranged around a coffee table with a bowl of candies on it. The walls were painted bright tangerine, the air-conditioning was humming, and the enormous flat-screen television was on, tuned in to the Beijing Olympics. Aco plopped down on the couch with the remote control in his hand to chat with Zoran and take in the action. I talked to Wendy, who unlike her husband was soft-spoken and reserved. Before we'd arrived, Zoran Sangut had clued me in to something else that distinguished her: unlike Aco, Wendy was a Croat.

They had met in 1991, only a few months before the outbreak of war, and their relationship had survived despite the conflict that threw a wall up between their people, which was no minor achievement. "Many mixed marriages have been wrecked by the war," the reporter Misha Glenny wrote of Serbs and Croats whose relationships split along the same lines their country did. Glenny also observed a pattern of "women assimilating the national consciousness of their husbands" in mixed couples that managed to stay together. I didn't ask Wendy if she would have stayed loyal to a Serb who expected her to assimilate his national consciousness. I did ascertain that she'd spared Aco from having to worry about the opposite problem. It was in her mother's apartment that the two of them took shelter in 1991, she told me, in a Croatian neighborhood where Aco's presence had to be kept hushed, something many Croats might have hesitated to do out of discomfort, fear, or something uglier than this. Neither Wendy nor her mother hesitated. When the bombing grew particularly intense and the building's inhabitants scrambled down to the concrete bunker in the basement, Aco stayed upstairs. Wendy didn't dare bring up his name.

As Wendy recalled this period, it dawned on me that, then as later, Aco had not been standing alone, but with a coconspirator who was as indifferent to ethnic nationalism as he was. As it turns out, there were other coconspirators. Though Wendy tried her best to keep Aco's presence in her apartment a secret, she told me some people found out, among them the Croatian couple who lived one floor below her. They had two sons who were serving as generals on the Croatian side of the war. Yet they assured Wendy nobody would lay a hand on Aco. One of the couple's sons was named Stanko—the man Aco later pretended was "Kovacević" in the cowshed.

There was, then, an element of reciprocity in Aco's story: he helped people who were vulnerable after having received protection when he'd been at risk. This did not diminish (or for that matter explain) the singular courage of his act: the Croats who refrained from ratting him out didn't risk their lives to protect him. Who knows whether, placed in his shoes, they would have done the same thing for a group of Serbian combatants? But it did suggest that solidarity perhaps did matter to him, not with the Serbs he saw behaving like animals during the war but with the residents of his hometown who had not been. As a physician named Svetlana Broz discovered while traveling through Bosnia in the mid-nineties, Vukovar was not the only place where such outliers could be found. In nearly every town and village she visited, Broz came across individuals like Anica Zečar, an elderly woman with Parkinson's who hid Muslims, Croats, and Kosovars in her apartment to prevent them from being ethnically cleansed. "Are there any Muslims and Croats here?" Serbian soldiers would knock on her door and ask. "No," she assured them. As Broz later wrote in the preface to a book of interviews translated into English and published with assistance from Harvard's Kennedy School of Government, she decided to set down the stories of people like Zečar "to reaffirm goodness as the ultimate postulate at a time of prevailing evil." The testimonies she gathered provide a moving counternarrative to the familiar tale of ghoulish savagery that served as the main story line in the former Yugoslavia, showing that even in an atmosphere of terror, when people were told they had no choice but to band together against their common enemies—in fact precisely because they were told this—some refused.

Of course, a skeptic might note that Broz's subjects were in the minority, and the skeptic would be right. For every Anica Zečar, there were far more people who behaved cravenly or reprehensibly, who let their imaginations be clouded by fears and stereotypes. But the human imagination is a peculiar faculty, capable of fostering blind hatred and prejudice, on the one hand, and of equipping people with the tools to transcend these forces, on the other. In her evocative book *Inventing Human Rights*, the historian Lynn Hunt contrasts the notion of "imagined communities" with what she terms "imagined empathy," a capacity to identify with the suffering of others that spread in the eighteenth century as novels and art awakened citizens to what they shared with people from different social backgrounds and that eventually sparked campaigns to end judicially sanctioned torture and other inhumane practices. "'Imagined empathy' serves as the foundation of human rights rather than of nationalism," argues Hunt. "It is imagined, not in the sense of made up, but in the sense that empathy requires a leap of faith, of imagining that someone else is like you."

The problem with this form of imaginative bonding is that, in polarized places, people generally stop taking such leaps, particularly when they cease engaging in dialogue with their presumed enemies. "Empathy only develops through social interaction," Hunt acknowledges. I kept wondering how a loner like Aco mustered the imaginative sympathy to take action on behalf of the prisoners in Stajićevo after spending months fearing that Croatian soldiers might find out where he was hiding and kill him—until I met Wendy and realized he had good reason to believe that, just as his mother had told him during his childhood, not all Croats were bad people. Near the end of my visit, I asked Wendy what she thought of Croats who disapproved of Aco because he was a Serb. "I don't care," she sneered. When I asked how she felt when he told her what had happened in the cowshed, her eyes brightened. "I was very proud," she said with a smile.

I glanced over to see if Aco had heard this and saw that he

hadn't—he was too absorbed in the television, his eyes glued to his favorite sport, tennis. Only he wasn't watching the Olympics anymore. While Wendy and I had been talking, he'd begun showing Zoran footage of his son, Ognjen, hammering ground strokes from the back of a court as a trainer fed him balls. Aco had undoubtedly seen the footage before, but you wouldn't have known it from his face, which beamed with delight. It wasn't the first indication I'd had that he was an involved—and adoring—father. On our drive to Vukovar the day we met, he'd spoken at length about Ognjen, telling me he served as his coach—"his moral coach," he'd taken pains to stress, by which he meant that he made sure excelling at tennis wouldn't cause his son to develop a swelled head or to neglect his other responsibilities, like schoolwork.

A year or so after my last visit to Vukovar, I learned that Ognjen's "moral coach" was finally going to be recognized for his conduct during the war: Zoran's plea that Aco be awarded a medal had been answered, and the response was, surprisingly, positive. When I heard the news, I briefly imagined a future when the divisions sown by the conflict faded and the children of mixed marriages like Ognjen would simply be brought up as citizens, not Croats or Serbs. Then it occurred to me that, in Ognjen's case, this was already true, and not only because of his father's influence. When I asked Wendy whether she had spoken much to him about the war, she shook her head. "Ognjen is a child, and I don't want him to know too much about ugly things. He knows some basic things and this is enough." What about his identity, I asked—in a town where children were sent to school in shifts segregated by ethnicity, how did he think of himself? She seemed taken aback by the question. "I am a Croat," she said after a pause. "But I am not some orthodox Croat. I am a normal person, and I have my family, and I don't care about Croats and Serbs."

3. THE RULES OF CONSCIENCE

It is among the most famous acts of resistance in history. In late July 1846, a New England writer, recluse, and amateur botanist named Henry David Thoreau left the shingled cottage near Walden Pond where he'd taken up residence to visit the cobbler's shop in Concord, Massachusetts. He was going there to pick up a shoe, but on the way bumped into Sam Staples, the local constable, who was responsible for collecting the poll tax assessed on all male adults in the town between the ages of twenty and seventy. Thoreau, then twenty-nine, hadn't paid the tax for years and, owing to certain personal convictions, wasn't about to, which meant he might be forced to take up residence in less bucolic quarters for a while. "Henry, if you don't pay, I shall have to lock you up pretty soon," said Staples. "As well now as any time," replied Thoreau.

Thoreau was taken to the county jail, where he spent the night in a small chamber with thick stone walls and grated windows. He was released in the morning, after someone, probably his aunt Maria, heard what had happened and dropped off money at the Staples residence on her nephew's behalf, for which some people might have been grateful. Not Thoreau, who a year and a half later appeared at the Concord Lyceum to deliver a lecture explaining why, had it been up to him, he might have settled in for a longer stay. "Under a government which imprisons any unjustly, the true place for a just man is also a prison," he proclaimed. Refusing to pay taxes in a country that tolerated slavery and had recently launched an unjust war on Mexico was not a crime but a moral obligation, Thoreau insisted: "When a sixth of the population which has undertaken to be the refuge of liberty are slaves and a whole country is unjustly overrun and conquered by a foreign army . . . I think that it is not too soon for honest men to rebel and revolutionize." Published in 1849 in an obscure journal called *Aesthetic Papers* under the title "Resistance to Civil Government," Thoreau's fiery speech attracted little notice at first. It would later appear under a more familiar title, "On the Duty of Civil Disobedience," and become one of the best-known ruminations on the subject of dissent ever penned.

Thoreau's essay has often been read as a stirring ode to nonconformists who put conscience above the letter of the law and the will of the majority. Yet it is notable that, for all his militancy, the author of "On the Duty of Civil Disobedience" did not call on his fellow citizens to come together to end slavery. He merely sought to avoid its taint. "It is not a man's duty, as a matter of course, to devote himself to the eradication of any, even the most enormous wrong," wrote Thoreau. "He may still properly have other concerns to engage him; but it is his duty, at least, to wash his hands of it, and, if he gives it no thought longer, not to give it practically his support." More than a century after Thoreau drew this distinction, Hannah Arendt cited it to highlight a distinction of her own. Thoreau's words underscored the difference between the "good citizen," who was concerned with improving conditions in society, and the "good man," who was preoccupied with maintaining his own moral purity. While good citizens waded into the messy world of politics, where absolute justice invariably proved elusive, good men saw politics as an expression of personal morality and little else, she argued. They could afford to be purists, since the only test that mattered was whether they'd been true to their own subjective sense of right and wrong. Thoreau did not pretend otherwise. "I am not responsible for the successful working of the machinery of society," he wrote. "The only obligation which I have a right to assume, is to do at any time what I think right."

It is a bracingly uncompromising worldview. But if this is all that saying no entails, what beyond salving one's own conscience comes of it? If one person's subjective values can be invoked to break the law and resist government, why can't another, radically different set of personal convictions? How do we judge someone who claims to act according to what he thinks is "right"? What if we don't agree with his principles? What is to stop the principled defiance of a "good man" from being emulated by a dangerous fanatic?

I. Beautiful Souls

During the course of his upbringing, Avner Wishnitzer gave little thought to the duty of resisting government. He was far more concerned with the duty of serving it. At the age of ten, Avner sat at home leafing through a photo album of the 1967 Six-Day War: Mirage jets streaking through the sky, portraits of Israeli generals, soldiers trekking through the Sinai Desert. The pictures made war seem glamorous, and filled Avner with a desire to be like those soldiers: strong, dust-coated, valiant. They also heightened his unease about what he feared he was—a gangly weakling with a gentle nature and an awkward build.

This would have been a potential source of insecurity for any ten-year-old boy. It was especially trying for one at Kvutzat Shiller, the kibbutz in central Israel where, in 1976, Avner was born. Founded forty-nine years earlier by a dozen pioneers who'd pitched some tents upon a hill just south of the city of Rehovot, Kvutzat Shiller had grown into a tight-knit community of several hundred residents. Splashes of pink and lavender bougainvillea dotted the lawns and flower gardens that ringed their modest bungalows, which were surrounded by eucalyptus trees and a medley of fragrant citrus orchards. By the 1970s, the utopian socialism that had inspired the kibbutz's founders had grown a bit obsolete, but a spirit of collective purpose still suffused the air, and Avner soaked it up. He came to like working in the fields, where young people were required to spend one day a week doing manual labor, and to internalize the idea that virtue was measured by what a person contributed to society, nowhere more so than on the battlefield, where the rugged sons of the kibbutzim had traditionally showcased their valor, shouldering the burden of defending Israel from its enemies. The residents of Kvutzat Shiller were leftists who voted for the Labor Party and believed in peace, but they were also patriots who'd long taken pride in serving with distinction in the Israel Defense Forces (IDF)—the more elite the unit, the better.

Things did not look promising for Avner on this front: he was too skinny, too gawky, too meek, a precocious reader with a sensitive streak. But, as his parents soon discovered, he also had an indomitable will. At age fourteen, Avner poked his head into the exercise room on the kibbutz one day, where a visitor from Korea was teaching a Tae Kwon Do class. He took the class, and came home to tell his mother he'd found an engrossing new hobby. She laughed. "Yeah, yeah, you're gonna quit in a month." Instead of quitting, Avner turned the hobby into an obsession. He got a blue belt, then a red belt. He trained almost every day. Three years later, he was anointed the junior national Tae Kwon Do champion in his weight class, his long arms hoisted in triumph after he'd won the last in a series of full-contact competitive bouts.

Though still a bit gangly, Avner was no longer a weakling, and he was soon invited to compete for something else: a place in the ranks of Sayeret Matkal, a.k.a. the Unit, the most elite commando force in the Israeli army. Famous for operations such as the 1976 hostage rescue in Entebbe, Uganda, when more than one hundred passengers of a hijacked plane were saved in a daring counterterrorism raid, the Unit was also known for a grueling training regimen designed to push recruits to their breaking points, a reputation Avner discovered was well deserved. Solo navigation exercises through the desert at night, nonstop physical and mental drills: the more punishing the battery of tests became, the more he hated it. Yet as his mother could have predicted by now, he was not about to quit. Like his father, a former paratrooper, he wanted to serve in a deep way, to risk his life for a country where ambivalence about military service was often perceived as an unaffordable luxury, if not an inexcusable vice. An idealist who yearned for moral clarity, Avner had no ambivalence. When he found out he'd earned the trust of his commanders and was being offered a place in the Unit, the idea of saying no never crossed his mind.

Avner served in Sayeret Matkal for nearly three and a half years. He was discharged in March 1998 and returned to Kvutzat Shiller, where he worked in the citrus orchards so that the kibbutz would pay for his education at Tel Aviv University. One day his older sister Tamar, a filmmaker, invited him to a lecture. Avner went to the talk, taking a seat in the back. The lights dimmed, and some slides were shown—cisterns filled with stones, damaged agricultural equipment, burned wheat and barley fields. This was the South Hebron Hills, a lawyer by the slide projector said, an area of the West Bank inhabited by Palestinians who were routinely harassed by Jewish settlers seeking to drive them off the land.

A right-wing soldier educated at a yeshiva might have dismissed the lecture out of hand. But Avner was not such a soldier. He was a liberal Zionist who'd entered the army in 1994, one year after the signing of the Oslo peace agreement, which like most people at Kvutzat Shiller he'd supported and assumed was being carried out in good faith. As the images flashed by, Avner fidgeted uncomfortably in his chair. Afterward, he decided to take a closer look, joining a convoy on a mission to deliver some blankets to a group of Palestinian farmers from the same area. The car he was in traveled along Route 60, across the Green Line, on a two-lane road that cut through the terraced hills and windswept gorges of the West Bank. It was headed toward Susiya, a village south of Hebron, but pulled to a stop a few miles before getting there, at a barricade where some settlers had blocked the road. A throng of Israeli police officers had also gathered at the makeshift roadblock and set up a barricade of their own. "This is a closed military zone and you're breaking the law if you enter!" one of them blared through a megaphone.

Some of the activists clambered out of their vehicles and started marching forward anyway. Avner lingered in back. He'd never broken the law in his life, and when he saw the police start clubbing the marchers, he felt paralyzed by fear. He also felt unnerved by the cheekiness of the activists on the receiving end of their blows. Why were these troublemakers provoking conflict? he asked himself. If the security forces—our security forces—were resorting to force, he figured they probably had good reason.

Had it been up to Avner, the marchers would have turned around and gone home. Instead, they pressed on, and the soldiers eventually let those who hadn't gotten arrested continue. Avner joined the procession that straggled to Susiya on foot. They arrived around dusk to meet their hosts, shepherds in tattered robes who lived in tents and caves, scratching out a meager existence from barren hills dotted with parched vegetation and desert blooms. The shepherds offered their visitors hot tea flavored with marwa and a tour of the destruction that had been visited on their land: wells choked with rocks, slain livestock, scorched fields. As Avner strolled around, the fear he'd felt before receded, and a profound sense of shame washed over him.

One might think that a soldier in the Israeli army would have grown inured to such feelings after manning enough checkpoints in the West Bank. But members of Sayeret Matkal weren't assigned such tasks. Other than a few months of basic training years earlier, Avner had never served in the occupied territories. Before Susiya, he'd also never spoken directly to Palestinians. The cruelty of what they described shocked him, though he still wasn't prepared to believe the army—his army—would knowingly allow innocent people to be mistreated this way.

But if the IDF's authority extended over such areas, why weren't the settlers responsible held accountable? Or simply restrained? In search of answers to these questions, Avner began crossing the Green Line more regularly, and the more he saw, the deeper he sank into disillusionment. Some time later, he was pruning trees in the citrus groves at Kvutzat Shiller with a friend. They'd brought along a radio, which ran a brief news item about a village near Nablus where settlers had infiltrated a Palestinian orchard and cut down two hundred olive trees. Avner listened to the report, looked at the trees he'd been assiduously tending, and felt a compulsion to do something. He proceeded to organize a bus trip to the scene of the settler incursion, a gently sloping field littered with the severed branches and hacked-up stumps of olive trees. As in Susiya, the army arrived to cordon off the area. This time Avner was in front, face to face with a young officer. As their eyes met, he felt a flash of recognition, as though he were looking into the mirror, at his doppelgänger. He wanted to engage the officer as a comrade, to let him know he was not some *yafeh nefesh*—the Hebrew expression for "beautiful soul," which in Israel connoted being naïve—but a kindred spirit. Instead, he found himself staring at a clutch of video cameras—the troops began recording the altercation as a band of settlers brandishing large sticks and M16s stood in the near distance, gloating. Avner shuffled back to the bus with a sinking feeling, realizing the soldier in whom he'd seen his reflection was just following orders, just doing his job.

In some respects, the awakening that Avner felt himself undergoing was familiar, even predictable: a liberal Zionist raised on a kibbutz completes his military service, attends a lecture, goes to the territories, and begins to register qualms about the misuses of Israeli power. There was nothing terribly unusual about this. But Avner was not just any ex-reservist—he was a member of Sayeret Matkal who still performed regular reserve duty and counted its members among his closest friends. His awakening to the plight of Palestinians also came at a curious time, coinciding with the eruption of the Second Intifada, the violent uprising that began in the fall of 2000, after the failure of the Camp David peace summit. In Tel Aviv and Jerusalem, suicide bombs were going off with numbing frequency, putting the suffering of Palestinians (and any thoughts of peace) far from most Israelis' minds. The murderous wave of grisly attacks prompted people to pull together, and led Prime Minister Ariel Sharon to order Operation Defensive Shield, a massive incursion into the West Bank in which twenty thousand soldiers were mobilized to serve.

One of those soldiers was a friend of Avner's from Sayeret Matkal named Moshe Vardi. Like most people, Moshe hadn't doubted the need for Operation Defensive Shield. But he'd assumed it would lead eventually to a resumption of talks. Months had passed and, instead, Israel's leaders insisted there was nobody to talk to because their generosity had been answered with terror. Moshe had gone with Avner on the trip to see the desecrated olive grove near Nablus, witnessing how little generosity many Palestinians experienced in their daily lives. Now he told him that several other members of their unit who had undergone similar awakenings were thinking of informing their commanders that they—the IDF's finest soldiers—would refuse to serve in the occupied territories ever again. Moshe was considering joining them, and had called to see if Avner might want to as well.

As we've seen, saying no doesn't always trigger a deep internal transformation. Paul Grüninger was a patriotic, fairly conservative Swiss citizen before 1938, and he remained this way the rest of his life. Aleksander Jevtić was a fast-car-loving, slightly lackadaisical resident of Vukovar before and after 1991. For both, what changed was the state of the world around them, not their ideas about it, which is why neither went through a prolonged bout of anguished introspection before breaking ranks. Sometimes, though, circumstances don't change much, but an individual's ideas and assumptions do. In these cases, the fiercest conflicts take place inside a person's mind and heart as commitments that once went unquestioned come to be reexamined and, at a certain point, betrayed.

During the first few decades of Israel's existence, few soldiers came close to reaching this point. For the generation of Israelis who grew up in the aftermath of the 1948 Independence War, the IDF was an almost sacred institution, a symbol of collective virtue that inspired unshakable loyalty and trust. The level of devotion declined somewhat after the 1973 Yom Kippur War, a joint attack by Syria and Egypt that shattered the army's aura of infallibility, leading to the resignation of Prime Minister Golda Meir. Still, internal dissent within the IDF was rare. Israeli soldiers didn't go around burning draft cards the way young Americans had during the Vietnam War. Most still placed undeviating faith in commanders they assumed would put their lives at risk only when the nation's survival was at stake.

Then, on June 6, 1982, Israel launched Operation Peace for Galilee, an invasion of Lebanon whose stated purpose was to bring calm to the north by dislodging Palestinian guerrillas from southern Lebanon. The real aim, it quickly became clear, was to drive the Palestine Liberation Organization out of Lebanon and install a puppet regime there. One of the officers dispatched to the front lines was Colonel Eli Geva, the youngest brigade commander in the IDF, the son of a major general who seemed destined to climb a smooth path up the chain of command. Geva led his brigade on a sweep through the southern Lebanese port city of Tyre, then up the coast to Beirut, at which point he abruptly resigned, telling his superiors, "I don't have the heart to look bereaved parents in the eye and tell them their sons died in an operation I felt was unnecessary." He was not alone. By the end of the war, roughly 160 Israeli soldiers had opted to go to prison rather than serve in a military campaign they had come to view as unjust.

So the spirit of Thoreau had reached the Holy Land, to the point that some of the "refuseniks" formed a group called Yesh Gvul—There Is a Limit. This spirit might not have moved as many soldiers in a more forbidding Middle Eastern country: Saddam Hussein's Iraq, say, where suspected deserters were routinely jailed or executed. But Israel was a democracy. It prided itself on having an army where rank-and-file soldiers exercised independent judgment. Soon after the Lebanon War, hundreds more began exercising such judgment by refusing to serve in the occupied territories during the First Intifada, when Palestinians marched, demonstrated, and threw stones in a popular uprising many Israelis concluded was justified.

The soldiers who did so were often pilloried as traitors and radicals, but they rarely looked the part. Unlike American conscientious objectors who grew their hair long and denounced the "war machine" in the 1960s, many of Israel's refuseniks were decorated combat veterans who'd proudly fought in previous wars. They hailed mainly from the Ashkenazi elite that had traditionally been overrepresented in the army's top units and senior ranks. They were not pacifists but selective resisters who took the IDF's claim to uphold high ethical standards seriously, which is perhaps not surprising. In his book *Obeying Orders*, the legal scholar Mark J. Osiel argues that soldiers steeped in traditional notions of military honor are more likely to resist unjust orders than conscripts with more jaundiced attitudes. He cites the case of an officer who learned of a recruit caught aiming his gun at the head of a Vietnamese woman and snapped, "Marines don't do that." In Osiel's view, professional pride and military idealism may prove a more effective constraint on soldiers thrust into morally compromising situations than abstract legal norms, an observation borne out in the psychiatrist Robert J. Lifton's study of Vietnam veterans, *Home from the War*. In the book, Lifton tells the story of an American soldier who was in the battalion that entered the village of My Lai on March 16, 1968, and proceeded to open fire on everything in sight—women, babies, elderly people. Throughout the massacre, which left more than five hundred Vietnamese civilians dead, the soldier pointed his gun at the ground to make clear he was refusing to participate. According to Lifton, what stopped him from firing was not a latent streak of pacifism but an "unusually strong sense of military pride and identification, a form of warrior ethos stressing honor; in Vietnam, and especially at My Lai, he felt both the code and himself to be violated."

Not all the soldiers in Israel who broke the taboo on refusal made a point of drawing attention to themselves. In fact, as time wore on, the army and many such soldiers found ways to reach tacit accommodations that suited the interests of both sides. Some conscripts did so by showing up at draft centers with a note from a psychiatrist diagnosing them as psychologically unfit for combat duty, a claim the IDF rarely challenged even though everyone knew it wasn't always true. Others engaged in a practice known as "gray refusal," which was equally discreet. "It's a deal of sorts that's designed to avoid conflict," the Israeli journalist and historian Tom Segev explained to me. "A soldier tells his commander, 'Look, I really don't want to serve in the territories, I won't do it.' The commander says, 'Okay, don't worry, in this unit you'll spend all your time sitting at this desk.' Then he calls his superior and says, 'Listen, I have one strange guy here—he doesn't want to serve in the territories. Let's keep it quiet.'"

In a small country bound together by a powerful collectivist ethos, the desire of such soldiers to keep a low profile was hardly surprising. It was also not surprising that even some people who shared their values came to wonder how much good they did. The primary aim of conscientious objection is "not public education but private exemption, not political change but (to put it bluntly) personal hand-washing," the philosopher Hugo Adam Bedau has averred. The observation would seem to apply to soldiers in Israel who quietly found ways to avoid standing at a checkpoint or raiding the home of a Palestinian family at night. A soldier who performed such tasks could at least try to influence the conduct of the operation. Opting out meant removing oneself from the picture—and, it could be argued, clearing the way for less conflicted soldiers to take one's place. The "beautiful souls" who chose this path might feel better about themselves. But what, in the end, would they accomplish? Wasn't it plausible that such principled noncooperation might make things worse? The "oldest charge" leveled against conscientious objectors such as Thoreau was "the charge of irresponsibility," noted Hannah Arendt, and, in her view, the accusation was often warranted, since conscience "is not primarily interested in the world where the wrong is committed or in the consequences that the wrong will have for the future course of the world. It does not say, with Jefferson, 'I tremble for my country' . . . because it trembles for the individual self and its integrity."

After fielding the phone call from Moshe Vardi, Avner didn't need anyone to run through the arguments against refusal for him, because they were so deeply ingrained in his own mind. "You cannot overestimate the power of the reservations I felt within me to this kind of act," he told me over coffee one day. We were seated in a patch of shade at a café with outdoor tables in Jerusalem, on a brutally hot summer day. Tall and lean, with close-cropped black hair and an intense, slightly brooding manner, Avner wore a frayed Sonic Youth T-shirt, gray shorts, sandals, and two-day stubble. His deep-set hazel eyes radiated seriousness. His voice was low and deep, and when he spoke, his thoughts unspooled slowly, in the manner of someone who studied a matter from every possible angle before deciding what to do. After speaking to Moshe about the possibility of refusing, he told me he had no idea what to do, and his uncertainty persisted through the meetings that he and a handful of other soldiers began to attend, emotionally draining discussion sessions that often dragged late into the night. "I was torn," he said. "I was suffering, really. Hesitating. We had endless discussions: What are the consequences? What will it do? What will people in our unit say? What will the media say? Are we going to go against many of the things we've been raised on, like serving?"

When Avner entered the army, he swore an oath of loyalty to his country and his commanders. All Israeli soldiers recited such a pledge at their induction ceremonies, but the bonds forged in Sayeret Matkal were particularly intense. The team leader he'd trained under was "something of a father figure" to him, he told me, the person who'd guided him through the bruising trials that candidates underwent. Avner had enormous respect for him. He also respected the view of his actual father, Rafi, who'd spent many years doing reserve duty in the Gaza Strip, even though he believed Israel should have withdrawn from the territory immediately after the 1967 Six-Day War. "He said, 'We protest—we vote, but we don't do these things through the army,'" said Avner.

It was a position Avner took seriously. He'd grown up believing what most Israelis did: that the army was above politics, that the oath of loyalty was absolute. Yet he'd also begun to think about the fact that, through all the years his father had served, the settlements kept growing. If this was merely misguided, a shortsighted policy that gave rise to the occasional abuse, disobedience was clearly excessive. After his first trip to the territories, Avner clung to this view. After a few more trips, he wasn't so sure. "I slowly realized these were not simply incidents—this Palestinian beaten, that olive grove cut down," he told me. "This was a system." The individual incidents started to fit into a pattern, in other words, and the pattern implicated not only messianic settlers but also the institution around which his identity was framed. Avner recounted the excursion he took to the desecrated olive grove near Nablus, where he found himself facing the young officer blocking access to the site as settlers stood watch. "The army didn't let the settlers come down," he told me, "but they were there with them. We saw the settlers with their sticks, and of course with M16s supplied to them by the state. And it was then I realized—it was clear to me that the army is part and parcel of what's going on in the occupied territories. It's not just the settlers. It's the State of Israel. It's the IDF." Something inside him snapped at that moment, Avner said, not because he didn't identify with the state or the security forces but because he did. "I could not say, 'This is not me,'" he explained.

"This is me," Avner continued. "The government was telling me that it was democratically elected and because of that I had to do what I was told. But what about with regard to the people I was being sent to police? They had no rights. They didn't vote. They had no way to participate in political procedures that could allow them to defend themselves."

As conflicted as he felt about whether to refuse, by 2003 Avner's view of the occupation had become clear. What he saw was not a misguided policy but a "fundamentally immoral system" that made a mockery of the IDF's claim to being "the most moral army in the world," an ideal he'd long aspired to fulfill. He could agree that soldiers were obligated to carry out orders they might consider misguided. But what about an order that violated people's humanity so blatantly that it bordered on being a crime? If an order was unlawful on its face, wasn't it his duty to refuse?

II. Black Flags

"If members of the armed forces commit violations by order of their Government, they are not war criminals and may not be punished by the enemy." So wrote the German jurist Lassa Oppenheim in one of the most influential treatises on international law published in the first half of the twentieth century. Oppen-heim would go on to draft the British Manual of Military Law, issued in 1914, Article 443 of which affirmed that if soldiers car-ried out inhumane and unlawful orders, the fault lay solely with their superiors. That same year, the U.S. Army enacted a similar code. Subordinates could not be punished for committing offenses "under orders or sanction of their government or commanders," it held. Lawful or unlawful, justified or not, combatants were expected to follow the orders they received. There was no duty to refuse.

This was the prevailing view among Western legal experts—until World War II, until the prospect of Nazis invoking the Superior Orders defense at the Nuremberg Trials prompted recon-sideration. The mass murder of Jews, Communists, and intellectu-als carried out by the Einsatzgruppen, the industrial-style slaughter in the camps: by the standard laid out in the British and American military codes, judges would have had little choice but to exonerate all but the highest-ranking perpetrators of these crimes, perhaps everyone save Hitler himself. But by 1945, the Allied powers had adopted a new standard. The revised British Manual code, issued one year earlier, held that subordinates could not claim immunity "if in obedience to a command, they commit acts which both vio-late unchallenged rules of warfare and outrage the general senti-ment of humanity." The new code adopted by the U.S. military stipulated that combatants who "violate the accepted laws and cus-toms of war may be punished." The timing of these changes was not an accident. "It was the historical experience of Nazi war crimes, conducted pursuant to superior orders, that led national and international legislators to reassess the relative dangers to their societies of obedience to unlawful orders and disobedience to law-ful ones," notes Mark J. Osiel.

Neither at Nuremberg nor afterward were the pressures that subordinates faced casually dismissed. "The fact that a person acted pursuant to order of his Government or of a superior does not relieve him from responsibility under international law, provided a moral choice was in fact possible to him," stated Nuremberg Principle IV. As we've seen in the case of Drazen Erdemović, the Croat who participated in the Srebrenica massacre after being told he'd be shot if he refused, sometimes a moral choice isn't possible. Most legal experts recognized that lower-ranking officers and combatants often faced demotion, imprisonment, or worse fates if they resisted orders, particularly in undemocratic societies, and that members of the armed forces were frequently given instructions to commit violent acts whose legality was murky. But while these circumstances could be cited to mitigate the sentences that defendants faced, they could no longer be invoked to evade responsibility for war crimes altogether.

Or so it was agreed when the victors of World War II sat in judgment of the Nazis. What would legal authorities sitting in judgment of combatants on their own side say? How much discretion and autonomy would they expect of them? How much should they expect? Among the countries where judges would soon be forced to grapple with these questions was Israel, where, in October 1956, on the first day of the Suez War, some border policemen arrived to enforce a 5:00 p.m. curfew in Kafr Qassem, a small Arab-Israeli village located in an area known as the Little Triangle, by the border of what was then the Jordanian-occupied West Bank. Everyone had to be inside by this time, the police informed the mayor of the village, a mere half hour before the curfew went into effect. Not surprisingly, the message failed to reach hundreds of day laborers who were still out working in the fields. When they started returning home later that night, the police began dragging them out of their vehicles, lining them up, and shooting them. For two and a half hours, staccato bursts of gunfire rang out. By the time the guns fell silent, forty-nine people had been killed.

Despite an initial media blackout, news of the massacre soon trickled out, and, some time later, the perpetrators were brought before an Israeli military court. Their defense rested on the claim that they had carried out the orders of their superiors, a convenient excuse that happened to be true. Hours before the massacre, officers from the Israeli border police had been summoned to a briefing where Major Shmuel Malinki gave them their instructions and announced that curfew violators should be shot. "What about women and children?" an officer asked. "Without sentiments, the curfew applies to everyone," Malinki replied, expressing the callousness toward Arab Israelis that was endemic at the time. (Until 1966, most of Israel's Arab citizens lived under martial law.) And people coming home later? *"Allah yarahmum"*—"God have mercy on them," said Malinki in Arabic, meaning that no mercy should be shown by the troops.

What followed was a textbook illustration of the situational theory of evil, it would appear. The soldiers at Kafr Qassem were not bloodthirsty sadists. They were ordinary men who succumbed to the pressure of the moment—the first day of a war, a climate of racism, an order to put sentiments aside. The situation explained the crime. Yet at the trial, testimony was heard from a platoon commander named Nimrod Lampert, who was dispatched to the neighboring village of Kafr Bara that same day. There, too, a number of villagers came home after the curfew, including a fifteen-year-old boy who appeared around 6:00 p.m. with some sheep. Soldiers brought the boy to Lampert, wondering what his fate should be; Lampert arranged for him to be escorted home unharmed. No killings occurred in Kafr Bara. Although he knew what the orders were, Lampert told the court that he'd spoken to the *mukhtar*, or headman, of the village shortly before 5:00 p.m., and that after this his "feelings" changed. In three other villages, there were also no killings, thanks to a company commander named Yehuda Frankenthal, who told his men to hold their fire. In the village of Tira, bloodshed was likewise averted. "I did not accept the order," Arye Menashes, the platoon commander there, told the court.

This testimony did not prevent the perpetrators of the Kafr

Qassem massacre from receiving lenient sentences—the longest, fourteen years, went to Major Malinki—but it clearly did influence the court. Orders that are "manifestly illegal" not only can be disobeyed, Judge Binyamin Halevy held in his ruling; they must be disobeyed. "The distinguishing mark of a manifestly unlawful order is that above such an order should fly, like a black flag, a warning saying: 'Prohibited!'"

Judge Halevy's ruling would soon be cited by another Israeli court: the one trying Adolf Eichmann. It affirmed something many victims of the Holocaust surely wished more Germans had demonstrated: that soldiers are reasoning agents, not reflexive robots; that being instructed to commit a blatant atrocity doesn't excuse doing so.

Far from finding the ruling troubling, the IDF embraced the "black flag" prohibition as an enlightened standard to be taught to all recruits. So, decades later, did Peretz Kidron, an Israeli reservist who, in the 1970s, informed his superiors that "as a matter of conscience and conviction" he would not serve in the occupied territories, becoming one of the country's first refuseniks (and, later, a spokesman for Yesh Gvul). As he informed me when I visited him one day in Ein Kerem, a neighborhood in southwest Jerusalem where he lived in an elegant villa surrounded by potted plants and wildflowers, he viewed his act as a straightforward application of the IDF's own ethical code. "When a soldier gets an order that is illegal, it is his duty to disobey it—the army actually set the precedent, they wrote it up," said Kidron, a spry man in his mid-seventies with a thick British accent acquired in his youth. Born in Vienna in 1933, Kidron came to Israel after World War II from Great Britain, where his family had fled to escape the Nazis; he went on to serve in the 1956 Suez War. "I'm a Holocaust survivor, so the idea of a Jewish army carried terrific resonance for me," he told me. For much the same reason, the idea of following orders that violated the rights of defenseless civilians—and international law—repelled him, he said.

But wasn't there a clear difference between an order to massacre villagers on their way home from work, which no reasonable person could justify, and an order to detain Palestinians at a checkpoint that suicide bombers had recently crossed, which plenty of Israelis would say prevented innocent people from being killed? Kidron shook his head. The army almost never court-martialed refuseniks, he told me, in order to avoid having to answer the claim that a "black flag" hovered over the entire occupation, whose legality was not recognized by any country in the world. "They don't want to deal with the black flag issue," he said, an argument Kidron advanced in his contribution to a volume of essays, poems, and testimonies by refuseniks that he handed me before I left.

Some time later, I put Kidron's argument to a senior Israeli officer. Nonsense, he said. "Look, the law is very, very clear in these matters," the officer maintained. "The time when it's appropriate to refuse is when your crime is a crime against humanity." And why didn't the occupation qualify as such? "Listen, to stand at a roadblock is not pleasant," the officer said. "To be a Palestinian at a roadblock is even more unpleasant. But a roadblock is not a crime against humanity. To stop someone at two in the morning and to take them from their kids, from their bed, it's not a crime against humanity, not until you know the context.

"Now, to kill POWs, to kill children, to kill civilians intentionally, to destroy hospitals or sacred places—these are crimes against humanity, and you must refuse," he continued. "Not just refuse but ensure that others don't do these things." The officer's belief in discipline and his senior rank did not prevent him from speaking frankly to me about moral lines he felt Israeli soldiers had crossed in the past. During the First Intifada, he said, the IDF had done terrible things in the territories—breaking people's bones, harming civilians—and the vast majority of soldiers had complied, much to his regret. "In retrospect, it's too bad there wasn't more resistance," he told me. "We might have woken up." But, he maintained, it was illegitimate for soldiers to decide they didn't want to follow an order that clashed with their political beliefs, not the least since, if everyone did this, the army would disintegrate. "In our army you need to leave all your agenda and political views out," he said, jabbing his finger in the air to underscore the point. He didn't even allow his wife to put political stickers on their car, since as an officer he belonged "to the nation," not one faction or sect.

Pulling a slip of paper out of his pocket, the officer showed me one slogan he did take pains to advertise: the oath of loyalty soldiers recited at their induction ceremonies, which he carried with him everywhere he went. "Always, I have it in my pocket. In every company commander's office, on the wall, we have a picture with all the signatures of the soldiers beneath this oath. It doesn't except orders—it says all orders that lead to the defense of Israel are to be obeyed."

III. Peace Criminals

The officer in question had, as it happens, recently disciplined four young recruits who'd taken it upon themselves to decide which orders to obey. The soldiers were in a battalion tasked with carrying out a mission in the West Bank city of Hebron, where several hundred Jewish settlers lived near the Cave of the Patriarchs, the burial site of Abraham, Isaac, and Jacob, surrounded by 160,000 Palestinians. For years, 2,000 Israeli troops had been stationed in Hebron to protect the settlers, who were not known for their moderation, routinely provoking conflict with Palestinians who came to pray at the site (which was known to Muslims as the Ibrahimi Mosque) and sometimes hurling insults at the soldiers, who were harangued for being too pro-Arab, spat on, or cursed as "Nazis." Yet not all conscripts lacked sympathy for these settlers, including some soldiers in the officer's battalion who learned their unit was being dispatched to remove two Jewish families from Arab shops that had been taken over illegally. The evacuation order came from the Israeli Supreme Court, but the soldiers were yeshiva students who sought guidance from another authority: their rabbi. He told them that participating in such an operation was forbidden.

The problem for these soldiers was not that an order from their superiors violated international law but that it contravened Jewish law. One consequence of the 1982 Lebanon War and the emergence of groups like Yesh Gvul had been to spread disillusionment among young Israelis from secular backgrounds. The vacuum this created in the IDF's top units was slowly filled by a new generation of religious recruits—soldiers educated at yeshivas who saw the Jewish settlement of the West Bank as a biblical imperative and soon began to question whether they too could disobey some orders, not to end the occupation but to preserve it.

One evening, I paid a visit to Elyakim Haetzni, a lawyer and former member of the Israeli Knesset who openly encouraged refusal on these grounds. An impish, portly man with gray hair, jug ears, and a high-pitched, slightly screechy voice, Haetzni greeted me in a white T-shirt and burgundy sweatpants at his house in Kiryat Arba, a Jewish settlement adjoining Hebron. We sat in his living room, where a large painting of King David strumming a harp adorned one of the walls and where Haetzni, sipping coffee and munching on cookies, held forth on the morality of disobedience. "Any legislation, order, decree, regulation, judgment, judicial decision, whatever, which rules out Jewish presence in the heart of Jewish land, in Eretz Yisrael, anywhere in Eretz Yisrael, is per se illegal," he told me, and had to be refused. I asked Haetzni, who was not wearing a yarmulke, whether he based this view on religious or secular precepts. The distinction was irrelevant, he told me, only that the core tenet of Zionism—"settlement in the land of Israel"—was being fulfilled. To Haetzni, one of the founders of Gush Emunim, the movement dedicated to establishing Jewish dominion over the entire West Bank, which he referred to as Judea and Samaria, there was no difference between Kiryat Arba and Tel Aviv. To remove Jews from either place was "a crime against human rights, ethnic cleansing against Jews," he said, "in the land of the Jews! Anybody who plans it, who implements it, should sit right next to Milošević in The Hague, as a peace criminal." He reached for a cookie and chuckled. "There are war criminals—I call them peace criminals!"

But what if a majority of Israelis decided it was imperative that Jews not settle land that the rest of the world regarded as illegally occupied territory? I asked. He waved his hand dismissively and, knowing I lived in the United States, cited one of his favorite American philosophers. "Ask Thoreau," he beseeched me. "What did Thoreau say? He lived in a democracy, and the duly elected democratic government decided to invade Mexico, right? And to practice slavery. Thoreau said those two things are unconscionable, although the majority supported it, and although this was enacted by law or decree or order—legally! Thoreau said, 'I don't pay taxes and I go to jail for that!'

"You come from America and ask me about this?" Haetzni sighed and, before I could answer, invoked the example of another American who'd defied majority rule in the name of higher principles, Martin Luther King, Jr. "We should go to America and learn from you!" Soldiers who refused to evacuate Jewish settlements were simply carrying on the same honorable tradition. "We are speaking about people acting under the command of their conscience!" Haetzni thundered.

We were speaking in a community that was home to a memorial park named after Rabbi Meir Kahane, the founder of the extreme right-wing political party Kach, which in the 1980s had been barred from participating in Israeli elections on the grounds of inciting anti-Arab racism. Some years earlier, a shrine had been erected to honor Baruch Goldstein, a Kahane follower who in 1994 entered the Cave of the Patriarchs and opened fire, murdering twenty-nine Muslim worshippers. Not long after visiting

Haetzni, I met a young Kahane admirer named Moshe Frumberg. Wisp-thin and freckle-faced, with six-inch side curls and a purple knitted skullcap on his head, Frumberg had recently been summoned to a draft center in Jerusalem to undergo an initial round of tests the army conducts for recruits. Before leaving, he and two friends hung a sign at the entrance that declared, "We Won't Be Drafted to Evacuate Jews!" Frumberg lived in Havat Gilad, a settlement outpost populated by so-called hilltop youth, who are known for their militant views. He'd recently passed his matriculation exams, he told me at the pizzeria in Jerusalem where we met, and in one course had learned that certain orders were inherently illegal— "like shooting your friend." These orders had a *degel shachor*—a black flag—over them, he told me.

"From my point of view, evacuating Jews is also such an order," he said, smiling earnestly and sinking his teeth into his pizza.

There was no right to disobey for zealots and fanatics, I felt like telling Frumberg. But there was also no way of escaping the inherently subjective nature of such labels. In the late 1960s, a network of American clergymen risked being sent to prison to help women get safe abortions, which in most of the United States were illegal at the time. Two decades later, a band of priests and ministers blockaded the doors to clinics to prevent women from getting legal abortions. Who were the fanatics and who the brave clergy of conscience? The answer depended on whether you viewed the decriminalization of abortion as a watershed achievement or an affront to God. A neutral observer might have argued that the opposing camps had more in common than they realized, sharing the streak of moral absolutism that often marked purists who put conscience above all else, including Henry David Thoreau. "If I knew only Thoreau, I should think cooperation of good men impossible," his friend Emerson wrote in his journals.

If the "only obligation" of a citizen was to do what he or she believed was right, why was Moshe Frumberg's act less warranted than Peretz Kidron's? Because Frumberg was driven not by universal principles but by sectarian religious beliefs, some might contend. But weren't many Catholics and Quakers who resisted the Vietnam War also driven by sectarian religious beliefs? Wasn't Martin Luther King, Jr., a devout Baptist? Hadn't pious Christians fired by faith often defied unjust secular laws in the past? In fact, for much of Western history the voice of conscience was simply assumed to be the voice of God. "A man's conscience was that inmost thought or feeling by which he knew himself to be in touch with something divine," the political philosopher Michael Walzer has observed. The original conscientious objectors were not secular humanists waving around copies of the Universal Declaration of Human Rights. They were devout Christians (in the main, Protestants) inspired by Scripture, which is why, in his original proposal for the Bill of Rights, James Madison included a clause stipulating that "no person religiously scrupulous of bearing arms shall be compelled to render military service in person."

Madison and the other Founding Fathers were students of John Locke, who, in his "Letter Concerning Toleration," wrote: "Nobody ought to be compelled in matters of religion either by law or force. The establishment of this one thing would take away all ground of complaints and tumults upon account of conscience." As Walzer noted, Locke was wrong about this: the line between religion and politics wasn't so easy to draw. By the time of the Vietnam War, conscience had become thoroughly secularized—along with Quakers burning draft cards were Marxists, feminists, members of the Black Power movement, devotees of Noam Chomsky and Benjamin Spock. And this, in a sense, is when the trouble began. Accommodating a smattering of Christian pacifists had been easy enough. Granting citizens of any spiritual or ideological persuasion the right to refuse to fight in particular wars, simply because it didn't line up with what they believed to be right, was another matter entirely.

Wasn't it necessary for good citizens not to impose their moral absolutism on others in a pluralistic society, particularly if there was a risk that dangerous zealots might do the same thing? So argued people like Yariv Oppenheimer, the general secretary of Peace Now. "I too recently guarded settlements and checkpoints contrary to my worldview," wrote Oppenheimer in an essay on refusal, which he opposed. "I did this, among other reasons, because I believe that one day, when the IDF will be instructed to evict an outpost or a settlement, a segment of all the soldiers of the IDF will take part in the mission, including the national-religious Zionists."

"Breaking the frame of the law is good when it serves your purpose, and not when it serves the purpose of the other side," an Israeli reservist acknowledged to me one night. He was Moshe Vardi, the member of Sayeret Matkal who'd called Avner Wishnitzer to broach the idea of refusal. With an arrow-straight posture and a focused gaze, Vardi did not seem to lack for resolve. Yet he agonized greatly over whether to refuse, he told me, and one reason was his fear that right-wing soldiers would do the same thing when ordered to dismantle settlements. "We discussed the question of what is the difference between our refusal and the right wing's refusal," Vardi said. "We came up with all sorts of points, but in the end what we could say is—this is refusal, and that is refusal. I don't entirely disagree with people who say it's the same."

Had Vardi been able to weigh the matter from a distance, I sensed from the hesitation in his voice that he might have decided against "breaking the frame" of the law. But he didn't have the luxury of distance, and the philosophical implications paled next to the personal ones. Vardi had children, and he told me he kept thinking about the future they'd be facing—and the questions they might pose to him—when it came time for them to serve. "I didn't want anyone to ask me in twenty years, why didn't you do anything?" he said. In the end, this is what led him to sign the letter that he and twelve other members of Sayeret Matkal composed and sent to Prime Minister Ariel Sharon. "Private exemption" was indeed not enough, its signatories agreed: their refusal would be as loud and public as possible. "We say to you today, we will no longer give our hands to the oppressive reign in the territories and the denial of human rights to millions of Palestinians," stated the letter. "We shall no longer serve as a shield in the crusade of the settlements. We shall no longer corrupt our moral character in missions of oppression."

Where Vardi thought about the future and his kids, Avner Wishnitzer thought about the past, sometimes while taking courses at Tel Aviv University, where he chose to major in history, other times while strolling around his childhood haunts. Growing up, he often hung out at a huge green storage house set on a hill overlooking the surrounding orange groves. The house was near Zaranugah, an adjacent Arab village where, for decades, no Arabs had lived. Avner and his friends would gather on the veranda to eat watermelon in the afternoons, spitting seeds into the gentle breeze that lent the ramshackle edifice its peculiar charm. It never occurred to him to ask where its owners had gone. Suddenly eager to know, he discovered that Israeli troops had destroyed the village in 1948; most of its inhabitants ended up in Gaza.

The grandson of a Czech Jew who'd been captured by the Gestapo before somehow making his way to Palestine in 1941, Avner had grown up devouring books about the Holocaust. He'd read nothing about what Palestinians referred to as al-Nakba (the Catastrophe), the mass expulsion that occurred in 1948. Yet it was not the history of the Arabs that preoccupied him as he contemplated what to do. It was the history of the Jews, in particular the question of how decent people managed not to notice what was happening to people like his grandfather. During one semester at Tel Aviv University, Avner reread one of his favorite books, Klaus Mann's *Mephisto*, about a theater director named Hendrik Höfgen whose career blossoms under Hitler's rule, which he tells himself is not his responsibility because he's only an actor. Later, in a course on twentieth-century history, Avner saw a film called *Monsieur Klein*. Set in Vichy France, the movie told the story of an art dealer named Robert Klein who is blithely indifferent to the plight of the Jews around him until a newspaper lands on his doorstep one morning addressed to another Mr. Klein, a Jew he learns is being hunted by the police. Slowly the art dealer experiences an awakening. After seeing the film, Avner attended a lecture about it. "The professor who showed us this film said something that made it very, very meaningful to me," he told me. "He said, 'Look, the biggest crimes in the history of humanity were carried out by very few people. Most people were just bystanders, onlookers. They didn't take part actively—they just let it happen.'"

The scale of the crimes was obviously different, yet as Avner mulled the dilemma before him, his mind kept returning to *Mephisto* and *Monsieur Klein*. "I realized there was no privilege in being a bystander," he told me. "There was simply no such privilege. If you didn't oppose the occupation, you were with the occupation, because you let it go on."

It was the stringent logic of a certain personality type: the ironclad idealist who was as exacting about his obligation to oppose the wrong being done in his country's name as he had been about serving it, or for that matter about pushing himself to excel at Tae Kwon Do. In morality as in personal habits, the gray world of hazy half measures didn't exist for Avner: as his mother had long ago discovered, once he set his mind to something, he went to the limit. Ambiguity didn't exist for many other Israelis at this time either, albeit for different reasons. The 1982 Lebanon War and First Intifada had divided Israel in ways that opened up space for internal dissent. There was no such space in 2003, when the escalating bloodshed of the Second Intifada led an angry, frightened populace to unite. Against the wail of sirens set off by the seemingly endless chain of suicide attacks, which were openly celebrated by

Hamas and condemned halfheartedly, if at all, by Yasir Arafat, Israelis' faith in peace unraveled. Even many people on the left lost their capacity to sympathize with Palestinians.

It was in this inflamed atmosphere of unrelenting terror that Avner contacted his team leader to tell him about the letter he'd decided to sign. It was a Saturday, and Avner spent the day pacing around, anxiously rehearsing what to say. In the evening, he finally picked up the phone. "My heart was pounding—I thought, My God, what is he going to think of me?" he told me. Avner strained to get the words out; the response was better than he feared.

"He said, 'Look, I can't agree with what you're doing, but I know that your mouth and heart are equal, as we say in Hebrew—and this I respect.' This is what he told me, and it was so meaningful to me."

The next day, at around 5:00 p.m., Avner met the other signatories of the letter in Ramat Hasharon, a town north of Tel Aviv, at the house of one of the soldiers' parents, in a middle-class neighborhood heavily populated by air force veterans, to watch the Sunday evening news on Arutz Shtayim (Channel 2), a popular outlet to which they'd leaked their story. Avner arrived doing his best to look calm, which is not how he or anyone else felt. "We sat there, and I'm telling you our pulse was like one-eighty," he recalled. "It was so scary." At 8:00 p.m., the program began. The letter to Ariel Sharon was the lead story. Avner had his cell phone on, and by 8:05 it had started buzzing, as did the phones of all the other soldiers in the room, a cacophony of rings fueled by an avalanche of calls from other reporters who'd gotten their numbers and wanted to do follow-up interviews. It was the start of a media frenzy that would land their names in every newspaper and TV news show in Israel, a scenario for which Avner thought he'd prepared himself. As he quickly discovered, he hadn't. The following morning, the letter was splayed across the headlines. On the Internet, all the Israeli news sites posted articles. Avner logged on to sample the coverage, scrolling through the "Talk-Back" responses from readers, a stream of vitriol belittling them as "traitors," "Arab-lovers," "faggots." Most were from strangers, but here and there he'd spot a note from someone saying, "Hey, I know this guy." He woke up to a fresh torrent of abuse and, a day later, to more of the same. Soon, he told me, "I simply stopped reading—I couldn't handle it."

He didn't fare much better in interviews. A few days after the broadcast on Arutz Shtayim, Avner was invited to appear on a popular TV program hosted by a journalist named Oshrat Kotler. He agreed, figuring it would be an opportunity to explain why, far from undermining Israel's security, refusing to serve in an occupation that fueled the rage of Palestinians would ultimately bolster it. Avner got to the studio, settled into a chair, and spent the entire interview squirming in it as the hostess hurled at him a barrage of questions impugning his integrity. "She did not interview me, she attacked me," he said, "and I have to admit, I did badly, very badly."

The physical courage it took to serve in Sayeret Matkal was considerable, but saying no to the army—exercising moral courage—was "ten times harder," Avner told me, because virtually no one approved. For several weeks, he stumbled through life in a shell-shocked daze. He compared the experience to leaping out of an airplane for the first time. "When you do the military jump, you're trained to jump like this"—he tucked his arms in close to his body—"and, once the parachute is open, after three seconds, you look up to make sure it has no holes and you follow certain procedures. Then you do the actual jump, as if you know what's going to happen because you've practiced so many times, and you're sucked out of the airplane and for three seconds you have no idea what's happening. Gone are all the things you practiced—it's only you and yourself, there's nobody there to tell you what to do. This is what I felt. We talked about it, we tried to prepare ourselves, but that eight o'clock news edition was the jump. And then for several days we had no idea what was going on."

IV. Purged

I had never jumped out of an airplane, or even been trained to load a gun. Yet sometimes, as I listened to Avner tell his story, I felt like I was hearing an account of my imaginary counterlife, the alternative path I might have followed had a few twists in my family history been different. Avner was born on a kibbutz in 1976. I was born in Jerusalem in 1970. His father had been a paratrooper, mine a corporal, but while his family stayed in Israel, mine had moved to the United States when I was two years old. Fourteen and a half years later, in the summer of 1987, on the way back from a summer visit to Israel, I was detained at the airport by Israeli officials, who apparently believed I'd been living there all along and was sneaking off to avoid military service. I was taken to an army base and interrogated by a surly officer who peppered me with hostile questions until an uncle who happened to be doing his reserve duty arrived to explain that I was not a deserter but an American.

An American with an extremely airbrushed view of the institution I was supposedly fleeing, he might have added. The move to America had relieved me of the duty to serve, but it had done nothing to diminish my admiration for the IDF, a glamorous fighting force I felt mildly ashamed not to be part of, as my father and grandfather had been. Whenever arguments about Israel broke out in my presence during my upbringing, I leapt to its defense, ticking off the dates—'48, '67, '73—when the heroic feats of its soldiers had saved the country from being crushed. A year or so into college, I lost some of the righteousness that infused my tone on such occasions. In the West Bank and Gaza Strip, the Intifada had broken out, and, on television, I started seeing images of Israeli soldiers exactly my age chasing after children and hassling civilians. For the first time, I thought about being in their shoes, and felt relief not to be. Soon thereafter came heated arguments about the IDF's vaunted moral standards with my father and other Israeli relatives, who no doubt sensed in my holier-than-thou tone what I was becoming: a *yafeh nefesh*, casting judgment at an extremely safe remove from the place where hard choices had to be made.

They were right: Had I been in Israel, would I have had the courage to stare my relatives in the face and tell them I didn't want to serve? To be regarded as a shirker of responsibility, a bleeding heart? Hearing Avner describe how difficult this was made me grateful I'd never had to find out. So did watching documentaries about Israelis like Shimri Moran-Zameret, a pale, bespectacled recruit who, at age eighteen, informed his mother, Marit, that he was planning to refuse serving in what he regarded as an "occupation army." In the film, we see Marit with Shimri at breakfast, a palpable chill in the room. We overhear her tell a local grocer that Shimri is about to enlist, brushing over the embarrassing truth. After Shimri is sentenced to prison for refusing, Marit sits at home alone, spilling tears, because, as she proceeds to confess, although she went through the motions of standing by his side, she unconsciously pulled away from him.

I saw the documentary at the Jewish Film Festival in New York. After the credits rolled, Marit rose to answer questions from the audience. The following night, we met at a café, where she told me her dream had been for Shimri to serve in a unit like Sayeret Matkal. What the film depicted was true, she said: her attachment to *hachevra*—the web of intimate social bonds that linked Israelis together—"was stronger than my need to be close to my son." She took a sip of red wine and gave a pinched half smile. "I found myself keeping a sort of distance from him," she told me. Eventually, as the film showed and as Marit explained to me, she tried to make amends by showing up at protests, speaking up for Shimri's cause, questioning her own assumptions. The questions were heartfelt, and her love for Shimri was clearly very deep. But the gulf between them was, to some extent, unbridgeable: what drove her to attend the protests was guilt at having failed her son, not her own convictions.

The army in Israel was a sort of family, and so breaking from it not infrequently ruptured familial bonds, causing soldiers to experience, and sometimes to relive, personal traumas. "The decision to refuse was my second hard decision," one refusenik I read about said. "The first was my divorce."

Avner told me his father constantly checked the website of a group that listed the names of Israeli refuseniks in the period when Avner was weighing his decision. One day I went to Kvutzat Shiller to meet Rafi, Avner's father. A fit, rangy man with a gravelly voice and wry manner that uncannily recalled Avner, Rafi did not deny sharing his concerns about refusal. "I told him, Look, I have a problem—imagine that every soldier decides what is the red line for himself," he said. But when Avner went through with the decision, he told me he felt proud, and the way he talked about it—as a consequence of his own generation's shortsightedness, which had launched an occupation that should never have begun—made it sound as though, if anything, the act deepened their bond, and perhaps alleviated some unacknowledged guilt of his own. Batia, Avner's mother, expressed similar pride. She was a person who went "with the current, even if I feel it's not so right," she told me in the kitchen of their home, a one-story dwelling surrounded by flowering bushes and a small lawn. We sat at a wooden table with a bowl of gleaming pomegranates on it. "I said to myself, he's a strong man, he knows what he wants," she recalled of the moment when she learned of Avner's decision to sign the letter. But she also said she worried greatly about the toll that refusing would take. "I told him, 'I'm with you, but there is a price.'"

There was indeed a price. Not long after the letter was made public, the refuseniks from Sayeret Matkal were summoned to their base, where, one by one, they were brought before their commanders, reprimanded for tarnishing the reputation of the unit, and told that if they did not remove their names from the letter in a week they would be expelled. None did, and so they were dismissed. After the meeting with his commanders, Avner walked around the base with his banished colleagues for what he understood would be the last time. On one level, he knew that he no longer belonged there; severing ties was nevertheless difficult. "To say goodbye was not easy," he told me. "It's part of my experience, part of my memories, my friends."

Two years later, Avner began to feel a nagging ache in his groin. He complained about it to his girlfriend, Hagit, who teased him about how little tolerance men had for certain kinds of bodily discomfort. He mentioned it to his father, a pulmonologist, who assured him it was probably nothing. The discomfort continued, so Avner made an appointment with a doctor, who ran some tests that explained why it hadn't gone away. Not yet thirty, Avner was diagnosed with testicular cancer. Before he was able to process the news, he was admitted into the hospital to have a cyst removed from the gland in his body responsible for the production of the male sex hormone. He spent several weeks recuperating at his parents' house, where he limped around like a geriatric and urinated into a bottle. When he laughed, a stab of pain shot through his body. At night, his mind raced with fears that the disease had spread. He dreamed of his own death, imagining his eyes hollowed out and his neck withered.

Since only one of his testicles had been removed, Avner was told he would still likely be able to have children. He drew comfort from a saying that was the motto of the Tae Kwon Do school he practiced: "Fall seven times and get up eight." But about a year later, in July 2006, Avner felt the pain in his groin again. He went back to the doctor for more tests, which revealed that the disease had spread. "Fall seven times and get up eight." Avner ran the adversity-defying phrase through his head while bracing himself for a second surgery, straining to hold his emotions together while feeling himself come undone. One night he rubbed the testosterone cream the doctor had given him into his arms and shoulders, and sobbed until daylight broke.

It was only at our second or third meeting that Avner mentioned anything about this. "I had cancer," he said, "twice." I was startled, not least since everything about Avner—his steely gaze, the muscles roping his arms—made him seem not just strong but indestructible to me. He was a level-three black belt who still practiced Tae Kwon Do six times a week, and also taught it. I asked Avner what kind of cancer. "Testicular," he murmured, eyes lowered. I didn't pry for additional details, and Avner didn't offer any, but the awkwardness of the exchange hinted at the peculiar vulnerability I imagined he must have felt.

As I later discovered, Avner had written a book about his experience, under the pseudonym Yoav Tsoor, a humor-laced account titled *Bay-tsay Haf-taah*—"Surprise Balls"—that doubled as a caustic meditation on the macho culture in which its author was reared. In one scene, the book's narrator thinks back to basic training, when nineteen-year-old officers barked orders at the "female herd" they had to whip into shape. "Do you want to become men?" they taunted the new recruits, their arms bare even though it was the middle of winter, their voices low and gruff. Real men didn't complain about the cold or speak in high voices, the recruits learned.

Real men, of course, also had balls. Lying in his hospital bed, the narrator mulls over this thought while gazing at the television, where images of the latest war flicker on the screen. Israel has just launched the 2006 Lebanon War, a land-and-air assault against the radical Islamist group Hezbollah that began with a torrent of confident bluster and ended thirty-four days later without achieving any of its stated objectives. What happened to the great army that fought so valiantly in 1967? the TV newscaster asks in dismay. Perhaps it's the excess of testosterone coursing through the veins of the generals and commentators, the narrator muses bitterly. The illness afflicting his body serves as a metaphor for the virus that has spread through his homeland and been left untreated for so long, which was, perhaps, a way for Avner to convince himself that he would emerge from the hospital stronger than before: purged of the hormonal urges that turned young men into macho warriors and nations into occupiers.

Avner first learned he had cancer in 2005, five days after thousands of Israeli soldiers were ordered to carry out another controversial mission: evacuating all Jewish settlers from the Gaza Strip, in accordance with the disengagement plan unexpectedly implemented by Ariel Sharon, the politician long viewed as the settlement movement's most loyal patron. Before the pullout, in an interview with the Israeli journalist Ari Shavit, Dov Weissglass, one of Sharon's advisers, singled out the refusal of decorated soldiers to serve in the territories as one of the factors that spurred the withdrawal. "These were not weird kids with green ponytails and a ring in their nose," Weisglass told Shavit, but "our finest young people."

Avner and the other soldiers in his unit could thus legitimately claim to have left a mark on history: by saying no, they had helped to convince none other than Ariel Sharon, the hawkish Likud leader who launched the 1982 Lebanon War, that at least some of the land taken over in 1967 had to be evacuated. Yet as the date of the disengagement neared, the refuseniks making the most noise in Israel were not soldiers like Avner. They were people like Avi Bieber, a corporal whose battalion was dispatched to bulldoze some abandoned houses in Gaza that the IDF feared anti-evacuation activists were planning to take over. After seeing an officer scuffle with a Jewish settler, Bieber shouted, "A Jew does not expel a Jew!" and urged other soldiers to join him in resisting the operation. He was taken into custody and sentenced to fifty-six days in jail. But his spontaneous act of insubordination made the evening news, prompting right-wing websites to hail him as a hero. A settlement in Gaza soon named a street after Bieber. Twelve soldiers in his battalion told their commanders that they, too, did not want to remove settlers from their homes.

It was incidents like this that led some Israeli officials to fear that evacuating Gaza would spark mass refusal. In the end, ninety-five soldiers were punished for disobeying orders during the disengagement, but there was no mass refusal. The event showed how strong the bonds of loyalty and discipline were in the IDF. Yet as the sociologist Yagil Levy subsequently documented, the smoothness of the disengagement owed a great deal to the meticulous planning that preceded it. Before a single settler was removed from Gaza, units with a high percentage of religious conscripts were distanced from the front lines; others were quietly relieved of their duties.

A couple of years later, these precautionary measures had largely been forgotten, but the willingness of some soldiers to disobey evacuation orders hadn't been. In October 2009, two recruits to the Shimshon Battalion filed into the plaza adjoining the Western Wall in Jerusalem to attend a swearing-in ceremony. When the time came to recite the oath of loyalty, they unfurled a banner proclaiming "Shimshon Does Not Evacuate Homesh." Homesh was one of four settlements in the West Bank from which Israel withdrew in 2005. Afterward, it had been turned into a closed military zone, which had not stopped some settlers from returning to rebuild it. Again and again, the IDF had dispatched soldiers to remove them, but the settlers kept coming back.

The members of the Shimshon Battalion who held up the banner were letting their commanders know that, if ordered to dislodge the settlers from Homesh again, they would refuse. The Israeli army wasted no time dismissing their gesture of defiance as "a disgraceful disciplinary aberration." Yet, a few weeks later, another sign appeared, this one suspended from the roof of a dining hall on a military base by members of the Nahshon Battalion, which declared in solidarity, "Nahshon Also Does Not Expel." Soon after this came a third sign, put up at the training base of the Kfir Brigade: "Kfir Does Not Expel Jews."

The army once dominated by the secular sons of the kibbutzim was now full of soldiers who saw disobedience as a biblical duty, a view shared by people like Rabbi Elyakim Levanon, the director of the Birkat Yosef Hesder Yeshiva, one of roughly fifty state-funded academies where soldiers divided their time between Torah instruction and military service, under a formal arrangement with the Ministry of Defense. "Many people who were in favor of the evacuation from Gush Katif"—the main settlement bloc in Gaza—"today understand that this was a big mistake," Rabbi Levanon told me. I asked him what would happen if the army ever ordered a large-scale evacuation of settlers from the West Bank. "This will destroy the army," he said. "The order to do it will destroy the army." He compared it to being ordered to eat nonkosher food. "If a religious soldier is told to eat milk and meat, what will he say? 'Because they're telling me, I'll eat it?' He won't eat it."

V. The Anxiety of Responsibility

"We are all conscripts in one sense or another," observed Susan Sontag in a speech reprinted as the foreword to the collection of testimonies from refuseniks that Peretz Kidron had given to me. "For all of us, it is hard to break ranks; to incur the disapproval, the censure, the violence of an offended majority with a different idea of loyalty." Yet, Sontag went on to note, "resistance has no value in itself." A Mormon could resist the ban on polygamy; a racist, laws prohibiting segregation. "Appeal to the existence of a higher law that authorizes us to defy the laws of the state can be used to justify criminal transgression as well as the noblest struggle for justice," argued Sontag. "It is the content of the resistance that determines its merit, its moral necessity."

Measured by depth and sincerity of conviction, perhaps there wasn't much difference between left- and right-wing refuseniks in the Israeli army. Measured by moral content, there clearly was.

One way to draw it out, it seemed to me, was by applying the standard Adam Smith might have proposed, assessing the ability—or inability—of those saying no to stretch their moral imaginations by putting themselves in the shoes of people who were suffering and extending sympathy to them. This is what Avner Wishnitzer began doing after going to the lecture his sister had invited him to attend, and it is why his relative indifference to the plight of Palestinians slowly turned into compassion and then shame. The moral imaginations of right-wing refuseniks like Avi Bieber were more limited, as I came to appreciate when, a few years after he'd made headlines for disobeying orders during the Gaza disengagement, I met him at the Crown Plaza Hotel in Jerusalem. Big and broad-shouldered, with a boyish face and a cocky manner, Bieber spoke proudly of how he had stood up for his principles. "I don't have to act like a machine, I'm gonna act like a human being who has a conscience—this is a democratic country," he told me, words that called to mind Thoreau, who in his famous essay on civil disobedience chided citizens for serving the state "not as men mainly, but as machines." But Bieber, who was born in New Jersey and moved to the West Bank with his family at age nine, had a less finely attuned appreciation of democracy when it came to some other human beings. His father and grandfather had been active in the Jewish Defense League, he told me, an organization founded by Meir Kahane with a long record of racism and violence against Arabs. Like Kahane, Bieber did not seem troubled by the idea of Israel ruling permanently over millions of Palestinians, because he had no capacity to imagine them as something other than a nuisance or a threat. "I think the Arabs are a bunch of crybabies," he told me, adding that he believed "the situation will end in all-out war"—a prospect he seemed to relish.

Then he offered a somewhat less apocalyptic, if hardly more inclusive, view. Palestinians in the West Bank could "work the land," he said, but "Israel would never let them become citizens," adding that the country "belongs to us."

Had Avner Wishnitzer cared only about his moral integrity, the occupation would have ceased to concern him. He had, after all, washed his hands of the situation, fulfilling what Hannah Arendt identified as the primary goal of individuals who engaged in Thoureauvian dissent. According to Arendt, the "rules of conscience" were "unpolitical" because they were "entirely negative":

> They do not say what to do; they say what not to do. They do not spell out certain principles for taking action; they lay down boundaries no act should transgress. They say: Don't do wrong for then you will have to live with a wrongdoer.

Arendt's description arguably fit Aleksander Jevtić and Paul Grüninger, two highly moral but otherwise apolitical men. It did not fit Avner, who after saying no—to the occupation, to his commanders—decided to say yes to a new cause. Two years after signing the letter to Ariel Sharon, he became a founding member of Combatants for Peace, a group of Israeli and Palestinian ex-fighters who put their guns down to promote reconciliation and dialogue. Joining the group filled part of the void that being expelled from his unit had created. It also brought Avner into contact with new comrades like Bassam Aramin, a Palestinian from the village of Anata who'd undergone a metamorphosis similar to his. As a teenager, Bassam was among a group of militant youth imprisoned for attacking Israeli soldiers. Hatred of Israel consumed him. In prison, he started watching films that exposed him, for the first time, to the calamities Jews had experienced before Israel came into existence. One of the films was *Schindler's List*. At the start of the movie, the thought went through Bassam's mind, "Why did this Hitler not kill all the Jews?" By the end of it, he was in tears.

Bassam left prison convinced armed struggle would never end the cycle of hatred and violence that kept claiming more victims, a commitment he maintained even as the conflict plunged his family into renewed despair. In January 2007, his ten-year-old daughter, Abir, was walking to school after buying a snack when a projectile struck her in the back of the head. She was soon pronounced dead, the victim of a rubber bullet fired by an Israeli border guard, witnesses claimed. Instead of calling for the loss to be avenged, Bassam worked with his Israeli counterparts to build a garden in Anata bearing Abir's name. He also pressed for an investigation into her death, which the Israeli police blamed on a stray rock hurled by a Palestinian. Shootings of Palestinians rarely prompted thorough inquiries, and when the Jerusalem district attorney's office closed the case, the matter seemed settled. Combatants for Peace organized protests to demand that it be reopened, and eventually it was. A Jerusalem court later ruled there could be no dispute that Abir was killed "by a rubber bullet fired by border police."

Through such activities, Avner assumed what seemed, on the surface, like a new identity, the former combatant turned dedicated peace activist—and, on occasion, finger-wagging scold, as when he would return from a visit to the occupied territories on Friday and make his way to a Sabbath meal with family and friends, a ritual with which nearly all Israelis ended the week. "I've just spoken to people who have been beaten up by settlers," Avner told me of these occasions, "and I want to explode. I want to"—he slammed the table at the café where we were sitting with his fist, sending a spoon hurtling to the ground—"I want to say to the people who are closest to me, 'You know, fuck you all! Sitting here filling your stomachs with good food and paying lip service to your being uncomfortable with the occupation.'" He twisted his mouth in disgust. "'Fuck you all. Do something. How can you not do something? How can you not act?'"

It was the frustration of a "beautiful soul" who found it increasingly difficult not to feel enraged by his fellow citizens, and who'd gone from being vilified as a traitor to feeling something arguably more exasperating than this: ignored. Once the cafés they frequented stopped blowing up, nobody wanted to hear about the repression and abuse of Palestinians, Avner felt. There were, of course, plenty of Israelis who believed the cafés weren't blowing up precisely because, after the delusions of the Oslo agreement were exposed, the IDF finally launched Operation Defensive Shield. Many other Israelis had simply lost hope and shifted their focus from the dream of peace to more private concerns. Against this groundswell of disillusionment, Avner increasingly felt like he was talking to the wall. "You know what *tarhan* means?" he asked me. "It's a tedious person who keeps repeating things over and over, and you don't want to hear it anymore. I'm this tedious person." He flashed me an embittered look, a look familiar to Hagit, the girlfriend who'd teased him about the pain in his groin shortly before he was diagnosed with cancer. They'd evidently patched things up, having since gotten married. A Ph.D. student with a calm, easygoing manner, Hagit told me she admired Avner's fierceness— most of the time. She recalled a Rosh Hashanah dinner at her parents' house that a cousin of hers from South Africa attended. At one point, Avner compared the occupation to apartheid, prompting a vehement objection from her cousin. A heated argument erupted, and didn't let up until the two of them left the table. "He's that way," said Hagit, shaking her head and smiling, "everything to the very end. And I like it, but it does make life hard. He doesn't compromise."

The Avner whom Hagit knew was not politically disengaged. He was a full-time political altruist, relentlessly attuned to the moral shortcomings of his society, gripped by a version of the guilt that the psychologist Robert J. Lifton told me hounded the soldier he'd interviewed who was in the battalion that carried out the My Lai massacre and didn't fire. "He never quite got over it, at least as long as I knew him, and he had great difficulty accepting any praise for what he did," said Lifton, "because he still felt guilty for not doing more to stop the slaughter. Because that was his inclination—the very sensitivity that is a source of moral imagination, that led this young man not to fire, can lead to intense self-condemnation." Lacerating guilt is not normally viewed as a healthy emotion, but, in Lifton's view, it can serve a revitalizing purpose as combatants reflect on the suffering they've witnessed and come to assume what he called "the anxiety of responsibility": a new mission to rid the world of this suffering and themselves of complicity in it.

Avner had clearly internalized this anxiety, which explained why, unlike Aleksander Jevtić, he didn't wake up in the morning, gaze into the mirror, and smile contentedly at himself. The brooding aspect in his carriage reflected the fact that, although he'd left his unit, he was still at war, not with Palestinians but with a society he felt was willfully blinding itself. Waging this struggle sometimes left him drained and furious. But it was also, I sensed, rejuvenating, enabling him to feel things he might otherwise have paid an equally dear price for trying to repress. I saw one other documentary about Israeli soldiers during the time I was getting to know Avner. It was called *To See If I'm Smiling*, and told the story of a couple of female conscripts who'd served in the occupied territories, among them a soft-spoken medic named Meytal Sandler, who'd entered the army full of idealism and was then sent to Hebron. The harshness of the environment unsettled her at first, but Meytal adjusted, and soon took to performing her duties, which included scrubbing the blood off Palestinian corpses, with an air of detachment, even bemusement. On one such occasion, a couple of female sergeants came by. Spotting a camera, Meytal said, "Come take my picture," which struck her as funny, since the dead man she'd been hosing down had an erection. Meytal crouched by the cadaver, next to a latrine, while a photo was snapped, and if a quiver of discomfort ran through her, you wouldn't have known it from the footage of her going-away party in the film, where she is shown dancing and beaming. She was no purist, no *yafeh nefesh*. After being released from the army, however, the glow wore off. Meytal started having trouble sleeping at night. She began drinking heavily and walking around in a trance, hounded by memories she tried unsuccessfully to blot out. In the film's closing sequence, we see her sitting barefoot by a window, smoking a cigarette, running her hands through her curly black hair and clutching a white envelope. Inside is the picture, which she's decided to look at "to see if I'm smiling." She opens the envelope, pulls it out, cringes, and then turns away. She looks again, more closely this time, and, eyes moist, says, "How in hell did I ever think I'd be able to forget about it?"

There was a cost to saying no to the army, Avner's mother had warned him. But there was also a cost to saying yes, and Avner had paid it in ways he wasn't even aware of long before breaking ranks. In the IDF, he'd learned to be tough, to lower his voice, to suppress the gentle streak that had compounded his insecurity as a boy. He had proven his mettle, and in the process shut part of himself down, the sensitivity that seemed to be a liability to him in the IDF. It did not seem a liability to Hagit, who, when I asked her what word best described Avner, paused, rubbing her hands together. *"Rach,"* she said finally, *"rach."* It was the Hebrew word for "soft," and it was clear that she viewed this not as a source of fragility but of strength—the softness that enabled him to empathize with people he'd grown up thinking of as enemies and, later, to come to terms with a disease that might have crushed the spirit of a former soldier too intent on suppressing his vulnerability and doubt.

About two years after our first awkward exchange about the subject, Avner brought up his bout with testicular cancer again, this time by handing me a copy of the book he'd written about it under a pseudonym. He didn't mind if I exposed him as its author, he told me. We were standing in the East Village in New York City, which Avner and Hagit were passing through en route to Seattle, where she'd landed a postdoc. It was a muggy summer day, and after meeting on Houston Street, we walked together to Tompkins Square Park, in the company of the newest member of their family, Rotem, the boy Hagit conceived shortly before Avner had his second surgery. The disease he'd worried might prevent him from becoming a father had ceased being a source of such concern. In the park, Rotem frolicked in the spurting water fountains while Avner stood watch. He was dressed in his usual attire—frayed T-shirt, gray shorts—and had his customary two-day stubble. Despite his jet lag and the sticky heat, he looked relaxed, happy to be with his family and out of the vortex that consumed so much of his energy in Israel. "You know," he said, settling on a bench shaded by elms, "I haven't read the news for four days. It's great."

I looked at him and had a hunch he would warm quickly to Seattle, perhaps even deciding to stay, a pattern common among Israelis, who, upon leaving Israel, feel curiously relieved to be away. A few weeks later, however, I got an e-mail. As I'd discovered from the memoir he'd handed me, Avner's grave exterior masked an ironic sensibility and salty sense of humor that surfaced in his writing. "Here are some preliminary observations [about America]," his e-mail began. "Everything is so big here. Most supermarkets are bigger than an average town in Israel and most refrigerators can house a medium-size Palestinian family. Give us half the parking lots of outlets in Seattle only, and we solve the Israeli-Palestinian conflict." He marveled at the warehouse stores where everything came in gargantuan "family-size packs" that seemed like a wonderful bargain, until it hit him that "you actually have to eat and drink everything you had bought before it gets rotten." Later he confessed that he'd tried American hummus, which made him yearn for the real thing. "I do miss Israel (just as I am disgusted at times)," he wrote. "I belong there, not here."

This sense of belonging came from another thread of continuity in his story, a love of country that had dramatically changed form but never really gone away, along with an ethic of social responsibility rooted in his kibbutz upbringing that made Avner sound, at times, like the patriotic soldier he once was. He was not unaware of the irony. "I believe you have to serve your society," he told me on one occasion. "I believe it's my obligation. And in a sense that's not very different from what I felt when I was eighteen. In a sense, I refused and then became active in Combatants for Peace for the same reason that I joined the army—for the same obligation, or *commitment*, that's the better word, to my society." Only now, he said, "I serve my society in another way, a way I believe will take us in a better direction."

4. THE PRICE OF RAISING ONE'S VOICE

On October 10, 2003, an anonymous letter was forwarded to the Office of Investor Education and Assistance at the Securities and Exchange Commission. "Since business scandals like those of ENRON and WORLDCOM became public, it is the duty of all Americans to speak up and denounce any wrongdoing of Corporate America," the letter stated. Its author was writing to alert the federal agency responsible for regulating the securities industry about another potential case of fraud, perpetrated by a financial services company that for nearly two decades "has reported to clients in perfect format and beautifully printed material of the highest quality, consistent high returns on [its] portfolio, with never a down year, regardless of the volatile nature of the investments."

Attached to the letter were financial statements culled from the company's 2000 and 2001 annual reports, which made the unbroken flow of high returns all the more curious. "These reports indicate untimely investment decisions, extremely high risk profiles, elevated expenses and no disclosure about the investment portfolio," the letter stated. The firm's activities "have been covered up by an apparent clean operation of a US Broker-Dealer affiliate with offices in Houston, Miami, and other cities."

The author of the letter, which had been CCed to the National Association of Securities Dealers (NASD), the U.S. Senate, and several newspapers, including *The Wall Street Journal* and *The Washington Post*, claimed to be well acquainted with the inner workings of the firm. "This letter is being written by an insider who does not wish to remain silent, but also fears for his own personal safety and that of his family." It was signed "INSIDER."

I. Suspicious Minds

Three years earlier, in Houston, Texas, a woman named Leyla Wydler had clipped a small gold pin to her lapel, slipped on her heels, and set off to work. On the pin was an eagle and shield, the corporate symbol of the Stanford Group Company, a broker-dealer based in Houston where she'd just been hired as a financial adviser. The job came with a $150,000 signing bonus and a spacious corner office at the firm's headquarters on 5050 Westheimer Road, a four-story brick-and-limestone building across the street from the city's sprawling, upscale Galleria Mall.

It was the fall of 2000 and Leyla, a forty-one-year-old broker, had reason to feel proud of her gold pin. In her store of not-too-distant memories was the tumultuous period when she was a divorced single mother with two young children to support, no job, and virtually no money in her bank account. Now she'd been rewarded for the skill with which she managed other people's money, by a financial company whose headquarters made the previous brokerage firm where she'd worked—most firms, for that matter—seem comparatively down-at-the-heels. "It is like stepping into another world," observed a reporter from the *Houston Business Journal* after visiting the Stanford building on Westheimer Road, which featured marble hallways, spiral staircases, and a five-star mahogany-paneled dining room run by one of the city's finest chefs.

Despite the posh surroundings, Leyla did not feel out of her depth at her new job. Poised, personable, and extremely hardworking, she brought a large book of clients with her to Stanford, investors whose trust and loyalty she had labored exhaustively to earn. Yet the transition proved more difficult than anticipated, albeit for reasons somewhat beyond her control. Leyla started working at Stanford shortly after the collapse of the dot-com bubble in the spring of 2000 brought the bull market of the 1990s to a halt. As the mania for Internet stocks subsided and the value of the NASDAQ plunged, the mood in the financial industry turned gloomy, and drumming up business became harder.

Most business, that is. There was one financial product Stanford sold that was unaffected by the downturn: certificates of deposit at Stanford International Bank, an offshore affiliate of the broker-dealer, based in Antigua, that offered fixed-rate returns of between 7 and 10 percent. These CDs weren't just lucrative but also safe, Stanford's clients were told—or rather, were supposed to be told. To spur competition among the team of financial advisers Leyla joined, an in-house e-mail circulated every so often at the company's Houston branch, listing the names of all the brokers and the number of CDs they'd sold. The brokers at the top of the list were invariably showered with praise.

Leyla was not on the receiving end of this praise, which, to Jim Lane, the branch manager who had hired her, could not have come as a great shock. Before she'd accepted the job at Stanford, she'd told Lane that she intended to keep the assets of her clients in the custody of Bear Stearns, through which Stanford cleared its trades, rather than allocate them to an offshore bank she knew little about—a bank whose deposits were not insured by the Federal Deposit Insurance Corporation, she hastened to add. An experienced industry professional previously employed at Merrill Lynch, Lane did not argue with Leyla about this. Six months after she got there, however, Lane was unexpectedly terminated. Soon after he departed, management ratcheted up the pressure on Leyla and other brokers to sell more CDs.

Leyla could have responded to the pressure by putting her misgivings aside. Instead, she pressed for more information about how the portfolio at Stanford International Bank was managed. The bank operated like a hedge fund, Leyla was told. If this was true, she wondered, how exactly could the CDs be advertised as safe (hedge funds aren't exactly known for avoiding risk, after all)? And how could they generate such consistently high returns? When Leyla asked to see a portfolio appraisal of the bank's holdings, she was told this was proprietary information that couldn't be shared. She did learn that Lloyd's of London insured the offshore bank. After a bit of probing, she discovered the insurance covered liability for Stanford's directors and officers, not customer deposits at the bank.

Leyla's probing did not go unnoticed. The first sign of management's displeasure came when she was moved out of her new office to a smaller desk. Some time later, she was called into a meeting with her new boss and warned that she had to produce more. On November 1, 2002, two years after she'd been hired, she was summoned to see management again. This time she was told that she was being let go. No explanation was given, and the decision was not open to discussion.

As stories of resistance go, what Leyla Wydler did to get herself fired—ask a couple of rudimentary questions, refrain from selling a financial product that failed to inspire her trust—seems rather quotidian. She did not doctor the papers of desperate refugees fleeing the Gestapo or mislead the guards at a prison camp in the throes of a bloody war. She was not thrust into an extreme situation or a disaster zone. It is in such situations, when bullets are flying and lives are at stake, that principles and convictions are put to the sternest test: when saying no is most difficult, and most necessary.

But there is another kind of resistance that is arguably no easier and no less important—the kind that arises when the stakes are murkier and the circumstances more prosaic. When it takes some imagination to envision that dire consequences might follow from doing what everyone else is. And when some people will think you're crazy or paranoid for stepping out of line—when, indeed, you might come to wonder this yourself.

Leyla Wydler did not think she'd been fired from Stanford because she'd gone crazy. Yet a part of her couldn't help wonder whether perhaps she'd detected trouble where there wasn't any. No regulators appeared to be bearing down on Stanford. None of the other brokers at the firm seemed terribly worried about the CDs she was reluctant to sell. Suspicions did arise in some quarters about the offshore bank, but they revolved around allegations of money laundering, not the CDs, and whenever someone leveled them at Stanford—a reporter for *Caribbean Week*, for example, in 1996—they were sued (and ended up retracting the charges). Meanwhile, Stanford was a client of Kroll Associates, a private security firm that companies often hired to reduce their own exposure to risk and fraud—what Kroll called "compliance and integrity services." A few years after Leyla was dismissed, Kroll evaluated the condition of Stanford's bank for a Maryland-based foundation, and issued a positive report about it. Stanford was also a member of the National Association of Securities Dealers (NASD), the trade group that enforced rules and regulations throughout the United States to protect investors from fraud.

Leyla was aware of this. Yet she trusted her intuition. She also trusted a friend of hers named William, a soft-spoken man with a watchful manner who, some years earlier, had hired her to work at the small brokerage firm he'd started. They stayed in touch and, after Leyla moved to Stanford, got together every so often on the twelfth floor of an office tower in Houston where William worked. At these meetings, Leyla often brought along copies of Stanford's financial statements and brochures, which were as pleasing to the eye as the firm's headquarters were. Seeing them stirred a sense of déjà vu in William. Originally from Mexico City, he'd first visited Houston back in the 1980s, when he was running an export-import business. The company needed to open a bank account, and one day William made his way to a high-rise in downtown Houston to meet a potential suitor. He took the elevator up to one of the top floors, where a tall, mustached Texan greeted him. The Texan's name was Allen Stanford, and soon after shaking William's hand, he offered him a slick, glossy brochure. In it was a picture of the bank's employees, smiling, a soaring skyscraper in the background, which lent the distinct impression that the bank—a couple of shabby offices with no more than half a dozen employees—owned the entire tower. William listened quietly as the tall, blue-eyed Texan regaled him with descriptions of various projects, none of which had much to do with banking, and then walked out. He decided not to open an account.

The reports Leyla spread out on a table at their meetings were no less impressive-looking than the brochure William had seen back then, and no less peculiar. One indicated that Stanford had invested heavily in the euro in 1999—the year the euro was officially introduced. The following year, Stanford had switched out of euros into dollars while somehow managing to avoid incurring losses, even though the euro's value had fallen sharply. By the end of 2000, the company had more than half its assets in equities just as the stock market was about to nosedive. A year later, Stanford had discarded many of its equities, again without recording losses. Year after year, the company's assets kept growing and its revenues increased, no matter what the market did.

These oddities were detailed in some of the financial statements attached to the anonymous letter that arrived at the SEC in October 2003. Leyla had deposited copies of the statements along with the letter she'd signed "INSIDER" in various mailboxes in Houston, wearing plastic gloves to avoid the risk of smudging the materials with her fingerprints. There was no hard proof of impropriety in the reports, no details about how Stanford International Bank actually invested customer deposits—which, as Leyla knew only too well, weren't revealed to the company's own sales representatives. But there surely were grounds for further investigation, she felt. Stanford Financial, her letter warned in bold capital script,

IS THE SUBJECT OF A LINGERING CORPORATE FRAUD SCANDAL PERPETRATED AS A "MASSIVE PONZI SCHEME" THAT WILL DESTROY THE LIFE SAVINGS OF MANY, DAMAGE THE REPUTATION OF ALL ASSOCIATED PARTIES, RIDICULE SECURITIES AND BANKING AUTHORITIES, AND SHAME THE UNITED STATES OF AMERICA.

In August 2009, nearly six years after the letter containing this stark warning went out, Leyla Wydler was invited to testify at a U.S. Senate Banking Committee field hearing in Baton Rouge, Louisiana, where Stanford had a branch. By the time the hearing took place, the only people milling around the company's headquarters in Houston were federal marshals. The five-star dining room, the private theater, the corner office she'd briefly occupied at 5050 Westheimer Road: all this had been cordoned off as investigators collected evidence about what was now acknowledged as a massive crime, a $7 billion Ponzi scheme second only to the $65 billion scam pulled off by the Wall Street investment adviser Bernard Madoff.

As at Madoff Securities, the crimes at Stanford happened in plain sight, with plenty of investors, employees, regulators, and reporters who kept tabs on what was happening at the company failing to develop suspicions, or, if they did develop them, putting them aside. Why didn't Leyla Wydler? I got an inkling at our first meeting, which took place in a conference room on the ground floor of the real estate company in Houston where she was working at the time the news about Stanford's Ponzi scheme broke. She'd agreed to meet me there after I'd tracked down her number and chatted with her briefly on the phone. In the conference room, Leyla sat down and pulled out a spiral notebook, and the interrogation began—of me, not her. What was my book about? Who were the other characters? What had each of them done? What had led me to this subject? Why did I want to know so much about her?

Dressed in a light blue blouse and dark slacks, Leyla was wearing silver bracelets on her wrists, bright lipstick, and dark eyeliner. Her thick auburn hair was pulled back in a navy band. She'd just celebrated her fiftieth birthday but looked ten years younger, an attractive, well-groomed woman with a bright smile, full lips, and a trace of circumspection in her dark, almond-shaped eyes. There was warmth in her smile and also in her voice, but what she mostly did that evening was not talk but listen, with the watchful air of a journalist sniffing the air for clues about her interlocutor. As I fielded her questions, Leyla jotted down notes, or at least pretended to—glancing over, I noticed she wasn't actually writing down much. What she was doing with keen attentiveness was observing me—my hand motions, my facial expressions, my eyes. Like a good reporter, Leyla appeared to be using the questions both to soak up information and to get a feel for who I was, to gauge my trustworthiness, a role reversal that left me wondering when I might get an opportunity to switch places and find out more about her. Only later did I realize I'd been exposed to something revealing: the work it took to earn her trust, and the inquisitive streak that, at Stanford as with me, impelled her to do some probing before agreeing to go along.

As I would come to learn, being inquisitive was not something Leyla reserved for reporters who randomly showed up in Houston to interview her. Her daughter, Adriana, later told me the story of how her mother had reacted to the news that she'd gotten engaged. "She said, 'Let's go drink a martini,'" Adriana recalled. The point of the drink was not to toast the wedding, however, but to grill the future bride: Did Adriana know what she was getting into? Was she aware there would be good and bad times ahead? Was she sure that she was ready? Was this really the right guy? "She's not easily convinced," Adriana told me, making it clear she'd been subjected to similar cross-examinations before. "And she has to get all her questions answered, and she has to really like the answers to those questions."

Demanding good answers before advising clients to invest in a financial product was, of course, standard operating procedure in the brokerage industry, the basic background research known in the profession as due diligence. In this respect, Leyla's story appeared to illustrate how, for people confronted with misconduct outside of a war zone or extreme situation, it didn't necessarily take performing a heroic feat of courage to resist evil and act virtuously. All it took in her case was being inquisitive, exercising discretion, doing her job—albeit at the risk of losing that job, and much else besides. As Leyla discovered, the reward for asking too many questions at Stanford was to get fired. The reward for selling CDs was a 1 to 3 percent commission on every dollar brought in, a lavish rate that could (and did) make a lot of her colleagues rich, as a report she'd recently combed through revealed. Drawn up by the court-appointed receiver tasked with recovering the money of Stanford's victims, the report showed that, in 2007, 161 employees at the company earned bonuses in excess of $100,000 for selling CDs. Twenty-nine of them earned more than $1 million. During Leyla's stint at the firm, teams from different branches competed with one another to ring up the highest sales. The team in Houston was called the Texas Tequila Twisters, she told me, and set a goal of having each financial adviser bring in $2 million in CD deposits per year. Eclipsing $1 million earned a broker a free trip to Antigua, where Stanford owned an airport hangar, a newspaper, a private yacht, and a swank restaurant called the Pavilion with an eight-thousand-bottle wine cellar.

For individuals caught up in the middle of an ethnic conflict or civil war, becoming an outlier requires seeing past the interests of the community, of the group. For a broker at Stanford, it required seeing past one's own interests, a form of apathy fueled within an incentive structure that made it extremely rational to think about your personal benefits and little else. This is what was hard at Stanford—not asking questions per se, but doing so in an environment where so much money was sloshing around and, if you played along, some of it could be yours. Later, when the fun times were over, when Allen Stanford was no longer a billionaire treated fawningly on television but an object of ridicule, an obvious phony, reporters would marvel at how he could have gotten away with such a scam. But was it really so surprising in light of the spirit of the times—or so unique? In the same decade that Stanford became one of the hemisphere's largest private financial institutions (valued at an estimated $50 billion) by selling fraudulent CDs, firms throughout Wall Street made billions by convincing people to buy abstruse investment instruments full of elaborately disguised risks passed on to misinformed or ignorant customers. The trickery in this case happened to be legal, assisted by ratings agencies paid nice fees to label pools of toxic mortgage bonds safe, which is not to say it was less pernicious. Wall Street's profits came courtesy of a real estate bubble built on another kind of deception—subprime loans made to lower-middle-class Americans convinced they were getting a terrific deal, with teaser rates that would eventually soar up and cause an epidemic of foreclosures.

This was neither sustainable nor responsible, plenty of people were aware, but as long as customers kept lining up, did it matter? Not to most people on Wall Street during the unregulated boom years that preceded the 2008 financial crash, and the same spirit of indifference prevailed at Stanford, which in a way was not surprising. As we've seen, human beings are most likely to feel their moral impulses kick in when the harm that will result from their actions is placed directly in front of them. The calamitous consequences of the reckless conduct that became routine in the financial sector were distant, conjectural, and, to most people in the financial world, not worth bothering about, certainly not while six- and seven-figure bonuses were being handed out.

Then, too, there was an element of group solidarity at work. If the person at the desk next to yours was selling a collateralized debt obligation or sketchy CD, why shouldn't you? Why be the troublemaker, the killjoy? "If you weren't selling, you started feeling like the ugly duckling," Leyla told me of her experience at Stanford. Like the subjects in the Asch conformity experiment who had to trust their judgment against the consensus of their peers, it also became hard not to wonder whether the person who might not be seeing straight was you. In December 2007, five years after Leyla was dismissed, Charles Rawl and Mark Tidwell, two other investment brokers at Stanford, resigned. Like her, they'd come to develop suspicious minds, not least when an operations manager suddenly announced that all files related to the sale of CDs had to be cleaned out (handwritten notes removed, sales material tossed) save for official documents. Rawl and Tidwell examined the accounts of some clients managed by a handful of their colleagues. In every case, the clients' accounts were performing worse than Stanford's brochures indicated the mutual fund they'd invested in was faring, which made no sense. Yet when Rawl informed his wife, a former schoolteacher, that he was leaving his high-paying job because of his concerns, the first thing she said was not "I'm so proud of you." It was "You're crazy!" Tidwell said his peers likewise told him, "Look, no place is perfect," and made him think he was "nuts" to resign.

And in a way, to give up a fine paycheck, to risk losing your clients, to alienate your colleagues, to disrupt your family, to pick a fight with a billion-dollar company, *was* nuts, particularly if you weren't exactly sure you were right and they were wrong, or even what exactly they were wrong about. For all their misgivings, Rawl and Tidwell didn't actually suspect the worst. "We had no idea it was a Ponzi scheme," Rawl told me. "Maybe this shows we're not the smartest people in the world, but the first time we even thought about it was when the FBI asked me if I thought it was a Ponzi scheme, and that was August 2008. And I said, 'No, I don't think so.'"

Leyla, too, said her initial worry about the CDs was that they weren't safe or insured, not that they were fraudulent. When she later shared her concerns with some of her clients after losing her job, most ignored her warnings to pull their money out of Stanford's offshore bank, apparently convinced her suspicions were misplaced. The truth is, Leyla wondered this herself sometimes. "You have to remember, back then, everything Stanford had shone," she told me. "When you see this company and it's so wealthy and they have offices all over the world—who was I, this little person, to question it?"

II. "American Values"

A hero is what many people would have said Leyla was at the Senate Banking Committee hearing in Baton Rouge, where her speech drew a standing ovation from the several hundred defrauded Stanford investors in the audience. That the company's victims felt compelled to express their appreciation was perhaps not surprising. Yet it's not unreasonable to think a more neutral audience would have joined in the applause, at least in the United States. Back in 2002— the year Leyla was fired from Stanford—a poll conducted by Time/CNN surveyed Americans' views of whistleblowers who risked their jobs to expose suspected wrongdoing. Nearly six in ten Americans said they thought such people were heroes. Almost three-fourths said they would expose criminal misconduct in their own workplaces.

These results appeared in *Time*'s year-end issue, the cover of which featured a photograph of Cynthia Cooper, an auditor who overrode her boss's warnings and launched an investigation that revealed a $3.8 billion accounting fraud at the telecommunications company WorldCom; Sherron Watkins, an Enron employee who was demoted for warning her then superior, CEO Ken Lay, about accounting improprieties; and Coleen Rowley, an FBI agent who sent a memo in 2002 to Director Robert Mueller assailing efforts to cover up the failures that led to the September 11, 2001, terrorist attack. Arms crossed, expressions defiant, the three women had been chosen as *Time*'s "Persons of the Year." "By risking everything to blow the whistle," wrote the magazine's editors, "Cynthia Cooper, Sherron Watkins and Coleen Rowley have reminded us of what American courage and American values are all about."

Whistleblowers are "born, not made," the consumer advocate Ralph Nader once quipped; they are a "breed apart," it is sometimes said. Yet over the past few decades, far more members of this peculiar breed have been born in America than other countries, leading some scholars to view outliers like Cooper, Watkins, and Rowley as products of their culture who act on impulses that mesh with certain broadly shared norms. The belief that people should be suspicious of authority, the reverence for individualism, the faith in self-reliance: all this explains why the term *whistleblowing* was coined in America and why the practice is more common in the United States than in other countries, the scholar Roberta Ann Johnson has argued. The evidence from Japan, a more group-oriented society where until recently an employee's unflinching loyalty to the company was assumed (and whistleblowing was almost unheard of), suggests that where individuals happen to be born can indeed play a role in determining how willing they may be to engage in ethical resistance. So does a study that compared the attitudes of 252 workers in America and Taiwan. "Results indicate that employees from the collective culture of Taiwan are more likely to indicate they would make an unethical decision that benefits the organization and less likely to openly question an unethical practice by their organization," the study found.

Viewed in this light, Leyla's refusal to be cowed by the management at Stanford and the initiative she took to compose a letter to the SEC was a quintessentially American act, a gesture of defiance that might not have taken place in a more hierarchical society where workers, especially female workers, weren't supposed to challenge their superiors, especially if they were men. Leyla happened to have firsthand knowledge of how differently such an act might have been viewed in another culture, because she wasn't born in Houston. She was born in El Salvador, the youngest of five children raised in a macho, patriarchal society and a traditional Catholic family. At home, she told me over coffee on the morning after our first face-to-face encounter, the voice of authority belonged to her father, an engineer who became the minister of agriculture in El Salvador and who raised his daughters to be courteous and deferential. Educated at a Catholic school, Leyla was not allowed to go out without a chaperone; she certainly wasn't expected to voice strong opinions of her own.

It was only after high school, when she went to Great Britain and lived for a year in a room facing the English Channel, learning English and roaming around on her own for the first time, that Leyla began to breathe some less constrictive air. She loved it there, and afterward, she decided to follow the path of an older sister of hers to Houston. It was a bold move, though not an entirely unexpected one, at least to Leyla's mother, who was born and raised several hundred miles west, in the town of El Paso. (She met Leyla's father at a country club in El Paso back when he was studying engineering in Mexico, married him, and moved to El Salvador before Leyla was born.) Leyla now traced her mother's steps in reverse, and although there were easier places for a young Salvadoran woman to settle, the unfamiliarity appealed to her. From an early age, she told me, she'd had a restless, adventurous side, a vague yearning to be pulled out of her comfort zone that Houston, a sprawling metropolis of gleaming skyscrapers and seemingly boundless opportunities, piqued.

Yet Leyla did not entirely abandon her roots. Shortly after arriving in Houston, she returned briefly to El Salvador to marry her high school boyfriend. She was nineteen years old and didn't bother asking herself the hard questions she'd one day pose to her daughter. The young newlyweds returned to Houston. Soon thereafter, Leyla gave birth to their first child, Adriana. A short while later she had a son, named Armando. Married with two kids, she had everything she was supposed to want. The only problem was that she and her husband turned out to be polar opposites. The more time passed, the clearer it became that the marriage wasn't working. Raised in a culture where good girls weren't supposed to get divorced, Leyla had no idea what to do. Eventually she swallowed her pride, packed up her belongings, and left, taking her kids with her to a small apartment.

It was the scariest thing she'd ever done. Yet the divorce was soon the least of her worries. A few months before moving out, Leyla felt a strange lump in her breast. She made an appointment with her gynecologist, who told her it was nothing to worry about. Leyla decided to solicit a second opinion from a specialist, who ordered a mammogram that revealed carcinoma in the left breast. Leyla stumbled out of the doctor's office on the verge of tears and spent the rest of the day drinking apple juice, eating soda crackers, and sobbing. "I cried and cried and cried for like six hours, thinking, What am I gonna do?" she told me. "I'm gonna go through my divorce. I have cancer. I'm gonna have a major operation. My kids—how am I gonna support them? How am I going to do this? I cried until my tears dried out."

While married, Leyla had enrolled at the University of Houston and gotten a finance degree. Before learning she had breast cancer, she'd lined up a job at a bank. By the time she had a mastectomy and left the hospital, the position had been offered to someone else. Divorced, unemployed, depressed, she was too weak to lug groceries home on her own and, after a few more weeks, too broke to buy her kids much of anything, which didn't stop her from trying. "At one point, I had one hundred and one dollars in my bank account," she recalled, "but my son wanted Mario Brothers so bad. I said, 'Okay, Armando, let's go to Target!' We went to Target. I paid a hundred dollars for his Nintendo and his Mario Brothers." She laughed. "He was the happiest boy."

Leyla let out a sigh. She put her coffee down. It was still painful to talk about this period, she said. But painful episodes in life aren't always shorn of redeeming consequences. As she spoke, Leyla's voice betrayed no self-pity. When she reached the end of the story, her eyes circled the room. Then she turned to me and said, "Do you know what shapes character? Let me tell you what it is: suffering. Suffering."

In reality, of course, suffering doesn't always shape a person's character for the better. It can make people indifferent to the pain of others. It can make them self-righteous or vindictive. But in Leyla's case, suffering proved fortifying, prompting her to shed the submissiveness she'd internalized during her privileged but cloistered upbringing. "I grew up very well loved, I was well educated, but there was something missing within me," she said. "It's because, my father, I don't want to put the blame on him but he was very conservative, very controlling. I felt I was not allowed to say what I thought because, you know, in that macho culture, to be a girl was to be submissive. I had these dreams, these thoughts, these desires, this passion, but I was so repressed."

It surely wasn't an accident that Leyla learned to be more assertive in a society where there was a bit more space for women to pursue their desires and dreams. Her marriage at age nineteen was the last major decision she would make to satisfy the expectations of others, and the springboard to her future career. It was after being on her own that she began taking courses to obtain a broker's license. She soon landed a job and made the most of it, to the point that, within a few years, she was managing $40 million in assets and earning a six-figure salary, the prelude to her getting recruited by Stanford.

Given what happened next, one might imagine there was one aspect of U.S. culture Leyla was slow to take up—"the love of wealth," which Alexis de Tocqueville identified as such a conspicuous feature of American life. And it was true that, unlike some of her peers, Leyla didn't view becoming a financial analyst purely as a vehicle for personal enrichment. That's because she viewed it as a calling, a way to help her clients—many of whom, like her, were from Latin America—make prudent investments in a market untainted by the corruption that flourished in other parts of the world. This perception was a myth, skeptics might have warned her, particularly as regulations were being scrapped and restrictions on speculation removed. But Leyla didn't think it was a myth, in part because she saw American capitalism in the idealized light so many upwardly mobile strivers from other countries did. Far from entering the financial industry on high alert for wrongdoing, Leyla entered it convinced that she, and in turn the clients whose trust she'd earned, needn't worry about this. "I didn't believe that there was going to be any fraud in the financial industry," she told me. "I thought it was so well regulated that there couldn't be any, that's what I believed. Because when you read those books, you see pages and pages of laws and regulations. Knowing your customer, understanding your fiduciary duty—that stayed in my mind."

It was an oddly wide-eyed outlook for a whistleblower to possess, or so I thought until I began dipping into the literature on the subject. In their book *The Whistleblowers*, Myron Peretz Glazer and Penina Migdal Glazer drew on interviews with sixty-four Americans who tried to expose misconduct in their workplaces. Like Leyla, most ended up doing so not because they suspected a lot of people in their profession were crooked but because they naïvely assumed nobody was. "Whistleblowers, we discovered, are conservative people devoted to their work and their organizations," the Glazers wrote. "Invariably, they believed that they were defending the true mission of their organization by resisting illicit practices and could not comprehend how their superiors could risk the good name of their company by producing defective products, the reputation of their hospital by abusing and neglecting patients, or the integrity of their agency by allowing their safety reports to be tampered with or distorted." In another study, the scholars Philip Jos,

Mark Tompkins, and Steven Hays found that nearly three-fourths of whistleblowers scored very high on a "socially responsible personality" scale, which measured things like whether a person believed in meeting professional obligations and working for the good of the team. Whistleblowers, they concluded, "exhibit little of the cynicism and disillusionment that often go along with political activism or dissent. They are, if anything, too trusting of the organization's willingness to respond to their concerns."

It took losing her job for Leyla to discover just how unwilling Stanford was to respond to her concerns. It also took being blindsided by a scandal that shook up the business community in Houston for her to see the dark side of American capitalism. The scandal in question didn't unfold at Stanford. It unfolded at Enron, the Houston-based energy giant that *Fortune* magazine touted as America's most innovative company six times in the 1990s, during which the value of its stock soared. Few financial analysts warned investors to stay away from a firm that seemed to epitomize the protean spirit of the high-speed Information Age. Leyla was not among the skeptics, and as long as Enron's shareholders kept profiting, nobody complained. But then questions about the source of the company's earnings surfaced. The stock began to tumble. By late October 2001, a share of Enron was worth $13.81, down from around $80 at the start of the year. A month later, Enron declared bankruptcy. Its CEO, Ken Lay, and president, Jeffrey Skilling, would eventually be indicted and charged with fraud, insider trading, and other misconduct, a fall from grace that was dramatic but by no means unique. Similar scandals soon enveloped WorldCom, Tyco, Adelphia, and other firms.

Leyla was stunned. "I was shocked—I was completely shocked, I could not believe that it was happening. When I started seeing that these things not only happened in Mexico or other countries—that they were happening right here—I was like, oh my God," she told me. We were now in her office, a neatly appointed room dominated by a large U-shaped desk that opened onto another room full of file cabinets. Leyla rose from her chair, plucked an accounting book off a shelf, and thrust it in front of me. "Do you know what it took for me to get my Series Seven license with two little kids next to me and being a single mother? Oh my God."

The pride of an upstanding professional—and self-made American—compounded the embarrassment Leyla felt. Then, too, it didn't escape her notice that so many of the clients at the company where she'd started working hailed from places such as Caracas, Quito, Mexico City, Bogotá. It was not by accident that Stanford had opened branches in these cities, running ads in local papers that offered prospective clients returns two percentage points above American bank rates. There was nothing obviously suspicious about this, particularly not to Latin Americans informed that Stanford International Bank was a subsidiary of a regulated U.S. corporation based in Houston and formally affiliated with Bear Stearns—with an eagle as its emblem, no less. Leyla didn't have to stretch her imagination to understand why this might prove reassuring. After the Enron scandal, which she told me made her briefly want to quit working in the financial industry, she also didn't need anyone to explain how easily even a well-regulated system could be exploited if enough people failed to speak out and alert the authorities when exposed to suspicious conduct.

It hadn't yet occurred to her that, even if individuals did take the trouble to exercise this quintessential American right, nothing would be done.

III. "A Piece of Nothing"

In 1970, the economist Albert Hirschman coined a term to describe expressions of internal dissent in large public agencies or private firms: he called it the resort to voice. "Voice is here defined as any attempt at all to change, rather than to escape from, an objectionable state of affairs, whether through individual or collective petition to the management directly in charge, through appeal to a higher authority with the intention of forcing a change in management, or through various types of actions and protests, including those that are meant to mobilize public opinion," wrote Hirschman in his influential and illuminating book *Exit, Voice, and Loyalty*.

In the book's next-to-last chapter, Hirschman argued that Americans were actually less prone to expressing voice in this way than citizens of other countries, mainly because they were so accustomed to dealing with objectionable situations by exercising a less taxing option: the resort to exit. In a frontier society founded by rootless pioneers and blessed with an abundance of land, people were used to dealing with problems that arose in the community, shop, or church by finding somewhere new to live, work, or worship, which obviated the need to vocalize dissent. "The curious conformism of Americans, noted by observers ever since Tocqueville, may also be explained in this fashion," Hirschman wrote. "Why raise your voice in contradiction and get yourself into trouble as long as you can always remove yourself entirely from any given environment should it become too unpleasant?"

There was clearly something to this. Yet Hirschman's book happened to appear after a tumultuous decade of roiling discord during which plenty of Americans got themselves into trouble by raising their voices in opposition to authority. It soon became apparent that, insofar as the willingness to expose misconduct in large bureaucratic institutions was concerned, he'd spoken too soon. The same year that his study of voice and exit was published, a detective named Frank Serpico leaked the story of rampant corruption in the New York Police Department to *The New York Times*. A year later, a U.S. military analyst named Daniel Ellsberg released a copy of the top-secret Pentagon Papers to the press, detailing the history of America's involvement in Vietnam and the fog of deception that had enshrouded it through four administrations (Ellsberg was one of the Pentagon Papers' authors).

"I think it is time in this country to quit making national heroes out of those who steal secrets and publish them in the newspaper," complained Richard Nixon of people like Ellsberg. But Americans disillusioned by the dishonesty of politicians like Nixon did not stop making heroes of them. The distrust of authority engendered by the Vietnam War and Watergate scandal, the growing awareness of health and safety problems at nuclear reactors and chemical plants, the emergence of public-interest organizations dedicated to holding large corporations and government agencies accountable: all this helped turn whistleblowers like Ellsberg and Serpico into glamorous figures, courageous truth-tellers who personified the adversarial spirit of the times and captivated the attention of writers and filmmakers. In 1973, Serpico was played by Al Pacino in a movie directed by Sidney Lumet. Meryl Streep was subsequently cast as Karen Silkwood, a worker investigating safety violations at a nuclear plant who was killed in a mysterious car crash on her way to meet a reporter. The role of tobacco industry whistleblower Jeffrey Wigand later fell to Russell Crowe, and of Erin Brockovich, the crusading single mother who exposed the Pacific Gas & Electric Company's poisoning of the water supply in Hinkley, California, to Julia Roberts.

Resorting to voice was clearly a good way to win the love of Hollywood. Whether it was a good way to win the love of the heartland was less clear. Despite their admiration for rugged individualists, plenty of Americans viewed national security advisers entrusted with clearances who then leaked classified information to newspapers as traitors, and cops who aired the dirty laundry of their peers as rats. The adversarial spirit of the sixties was destructive, a lot of people felt. By speaking to the *Times* about the corruption he'd witnessed on the force, some critics charged, Frank Serpico helped instigate public hearings that tarnished the reputation of the entire NYPD. By pursuing an independent investigation of the accounting methods at WorldCom, Cynthia Cooper put everyone around her (including employees and shareholders unaware of the misconduct) at risk. Less than a month after she unveiled her findings, WorldCom filed for bankruptcy. The lives of thousands of people were upended. In the eyes of some, a disloyal troublemaker had acted inexcusably.

It is true that, as Roberta Ann Johnson has noted, "in the United States, people blow the whistle on waste, fraud, and abuse more than anywhere else in the world." But it is also true that Americans prize loyalty and that many regard certain forms of deference—to God, to country, to the rule of law—as sacrosanct. Drawing on data collected by the World Value Surveys and other sources over multiple years, the sociologist Claude Fischer sought to measure how sympathetic to rule-defying nonconformists Americans actually are. "In general, would you say that people should obey the law without exception, or are there exceptional occasions on which people should follow their consciences even if it means breaking the law?" citizens from nine different countries were asked in 2006 by the International Social Survey Programme. Forty-five percent of Americans said people should on occasion follow their consciences, which thus ranked the United States last on the list, below countries such as Sweden and France. "Right or wrong should be a matter of personal conscience," another survey proposed to citizens in seven different countries; Americans were next to last in concurring with this sentiment. Compared with Europeans, Fischer found, U.S. citizens "consistently answer in a way that favors the group over the individual," confirming Tocqueville's impression that a powerful current of conformity ran through American life. According to Fischer, Americans were "much more likely than Europeans to say that employees should follow a boss's orders even if the boss is wrong," more likely "to defer to church leaders and to insist on abiding by the law" and "to believe that individuals should go along and get along."

How could this be true of a country that assigned Thoreau's "On Civil Disobedience" to high school students and prided itself on its tradition of freedom and dissent? Part of the answer surely rested in the fact that, precisely because it was so free and open, many Americans viewed expressions of dissent as superfluous—or, worse, indulgent, an abuse of the tolerance and liberty for which citizens ought to be grateful. In part, too, it was because, as the survey cited by Fischer showed, a higher proportion of U.S. citizens agreed that "people should support their country even if the country is in the wrong" than in any other nation, which is why many felt little sympathy for people like Daniel Ellsberg and Bradley Manning, a U.S. army soldier accused of leaking classified national security documents to the antisecrecy organization Wikileaks in 2010, several decades after Ellsberg supplied the Pentagon Papers to the press. The documents Manning allegedly leaked included field reports from the war in Iraq, where he had been deployed and about which he had grown bitterly disillusioned, as well as a vast trove of diplomatic cables revealing what he'd come to view as the "criminal political backdealings" of U.S. foreign policy officials. In response, Manning was arrested for "aiding the enemy," a capital offense, and sent to a Marine Corps brig, where he was held in solitary confinement for nearly nine months—exactly the punishment he deserved for causing his country such trouble, many Americans informed of what he'd done might well have agreed. (Government prosecutors said they would not recommend the death penalty, but Manning still faced the prospect of being sentenced to prison for life.)

"Whistleblowers personify valid but conflicted values that are deeply ingrained in most cultures," Tom Devine, the legal director of the Government Accountability Project, a whistleblower protection and advocacy group, told me. "We're all raised to be team players and to be cooperative. We don't like people who are naysayers, troublemakers. We also don't like tattletales, rats, squealers—there's an instinctual contempt for those folks. On the other hand, we don't respect bureaucratic sheep or people who say, 'Well, I'm not going to get involved, because there's nothing in it for me.'"

Nobody called Leyla a naysayer on the day she was fired from Stanford. Instead, a broker who saw her getting escorted out of the building after clearing out her desk came up to her and gave her a hug. "Leyla, you know I love you, don't worry, I'll help you out," the broker told her. Soon after that, Stanford confiscated Leyla's Bear Stearns account, divided her clients among her former colleagues, and filed a claim with the NASD demanding that she return a significant portion of her signing bonus, which in their original agreement had been forgivable in five years.

By this point, Leyla's daughter, Adriana, was a sophomore at the University of Texas, in Austin. Her son, Armando, was nearing the end of high school. She had a mortgage to pay on the home she'd purchased, a two-story redbrick house in the suburbs shaded by pines. Suddenly all the old fears about how to support herself and her children came flooding back. Despite the parting hug, none of her former coworkers contacted her to offer support as she scrambled to figure out what to do. They were apparently too busy selling her former clients CDs, as Leyla discovered after calling some of them to explain why she'd had to leave Stanford and was no longer their broker. Leyla felt deeply betrayed. But she did not lose hope. After consulting a lawyer, she decided to file a counterclaim for wrongful termination with the NASD. Around the same time, she mailed off her anonymous letter to alert the media and SEC. "I thought, okay, I'm gonna fight this," she told me. Once the facts came out, she would prevail, she was convinced, because the system worked.

Some time later, Leyla drove to a building near the Galleria Mall, not far from Stanford's headquarters, and made her way up to a conference room. Before a three-person NASD arbitration panel, she told her story: about the relentless pressure she'd been under to sell CDs, about Stanford's refusal to provide her with a portfolio appraisal of the offshore bank, about her concern that investors were being deceived. Leyla had prepared hard for the hearing. She was extremely nervous. She thought it was odd that the arbitrators asked so few questions and stared somewhat blankly at her as she spoke, but left in good spirits. Some weeks passed. Then, on September 15, 2004, the NASD issued a ruling, dismissing her counterclaim and ordering her to pay Stanford $107,782 in compensatory damages—money she didn't have. Leyla had thirty days to comply with the order or have her license suspended.

So much for embodying American courage and values: Leyla's reward for displaying her individualism and refusing to be submissive at Stanford was to be chased out of her industry. After her case was dismissed, she felt like "a piece of nothing," she told me, a nuisance nobody wanted to hear from, while Stanford continued luring in clients and flying its top producers to the Caribbean. "My arbitration case—they probably went like this with it," she told me in her office, lifting a pamphlet off her desk and waving it over the garbage can. She smiled bitterly. "That made me so furious—I was trembling." Later, she would learn that NASD arbitrators routinely shuffled back and forth from the regulatory agency to the industry they were supposed to regulate. Among those to pass through the revolving doors was Bernie Young, who worked at the NASD from 1984 to 2003 and served as district director of its Dallas office. He would go on to serve as the compliance officer at Stanford's brokerage house.

A dramatic confrontation, a struggle to expose the truth, a David-versus-Goliath battle in which justice ultimately prevails: Leyla's story had not exactly followed the script reserved for whistleblowers in Hollywood. In the movie *Erin Brockovich*, not only must Pacific Gas & Electric fork out hundreds of millions in damages to its victims, but the sassy whistleblower played by Julia Roberts who took up their cause also pockets a million-dollar bonus. "She brought a small town to its feet and a huge company to its knees," proclaims the caption on the DVD of the film, which is how whistleblower stories were supposed to turn out.

The reality was slightly different, as documented by C. Fred Alford in his book *Whistleblowers: Broken Lives and Organizational Power*. "Among the whistleblowers I worked with, a little over two-thirds lost their jobs," wrote Alford. "Most lost their houses. Many lost their families." Depression and alcoholism were common; so was bankruptcy. It was different for employees with high seniority or rank, some might assume. But studies showed it wasn't different. Nor were the consequences less dire for government workers who were able to present their allegations in federal court, notwithstanding legislation passed by Congress to protect them from reprisal. "Whistleblowers have won only four of almost ten thousand cases to reach the federal courts under the Whistleblower Protection Act of 1989," wrote Alford. He told the story of a worker who spent $100,000 to get a federal judge to hear her case. "I had my day in court, only it wasn't a day, but a few minutes," she told Alford. "The judge said I didn't have standing to sue, and I was back on the street a hundred thousand dollars poorer."

Alford's book appeared in 2001. One year later, a man named David Welch attended a meeting in Charlottesville sponsored by the Virginia Bankers Association. At the time, Welch was the chief financial officer at a small bank in Floyd, a town of four hundred people, with a single stoplight, nestled in the hills of southwest Virginia. Welch lived on a nearby farm, on twenty-two acres of rolling woodland purchased from his wife's grandparents. He was a devout Christian and a perennial straight shooter whose wife sometimes joked, "If you don't want Dave's honest opinion, you better not ask him." At the meeting, Welch heard a presentation about the Sarbanes-Oxley Act, which had just been signed into law by President George W. Bush in the wake of the Enron and WorldCom scandals to prevent future outbreaks of corporate fraud. Under the new law, the penalty for certifying improper financial statements could run as high as $5 million and twenty years in prison, Welch learned.

Two weeks after attending this meeting, Welch refused to

certify the financial statements placed on his desk, having noticed irregularities, including recovered loans improperly booked as income, that he was convinced made his bank look like it was performing better than it was. On September 20, 2002, at a meeting with his colleagues, Welch went through the provisions of Sarbanes-Oxley and laid out what he felt was his fiduciary responsibility. He brought a tape recorder to the meeting, which the bank's CEO tried to turn off. Welch kept it running. Later that day, a bank employee dropped off a memo at Welch's home, summoning him to a meeting to discuss "internal Company matters" and specifying that he would not be permitted to have outside counsel present. Unable to reach his attorney for legal advice in time, Welch requested a delay. Shortly thereafter, he was suspended indefinitely.

Welch's employer, a unit of Cardinal Bankshares, claimed he was suspended for not showing up at the meeting. The bank also maintained that his allegations had no material basis. Welch insisted otherwise and filed a complaint with the Department of Labor, taking advantage of a landmark provision in the Sarbanes-Oxley Act that granted corporate whistleblowers the right to sue their employers if subjected to unwarranted reprisals. Welch's case came before an administrative law judge who, after sifting through the evidence, ruled that an "adverse and discriminatory employment action" had taken place and ordered that he be reinstated.

Thanks to Congress and President Bush, employees who spoke out finally had some protections. Or so Welch thought until his case was appealed to the Administrative Review Board (ARB), the federal agency that had the final say in such matters. As in the overwhelming majority of corporate whistleblower cases that came before it in the years after the Enron and WorldCom meltdowns, the ARB ruled against Welch, claiming he had failed to demonstrate why he "reasonably believed" the bank had breached a specific law in misstating its financial condition and that his allegations did not entail a violation of federal securities laws. This was in

May 2007, more than three years after the initial ruling in his case. As the dispute dragged on, the American Bankers Association and the Virginia Association of Community Banks filed amicus briefs on behalf of Cardinal. Unable to find another job in an industry he was convinced had blackballed him, Welch ended up moving to Ohio to teach accounting.

"I am fiscally and socially conservative, I've always leaned toward the Republican Party," Welch told me. "But I was very, very disappointed by many things that happened during the Bush administration." One of these things was his discovery that under Bush the ARB had been staffed with judges who seemed determined to gut the law he thought protected employees who took the trouble to report misconduct. According to *The Wall Street Journal*, of 1,273 complaints filed between 2002 and 2008, the government had ruled in favor of whistleblowers 17 times. Another 841 complaints were dismissed before being heard, sometimes because of minor technicalities, other times because employees worked at the private subsidiaries of publicly traded companies, which the Department of Labor decided were not covered by the statute.

IV. "No One Would Listen"

On the evening of April 20, 2010, just before 10:00 local time, a massive explosion sent a giant fireball shooting into the sky on an oil rig forty miles off the coast of Louisiana. The blast incinerated eleven workers and soon blackened coastlines, befouled wetlands, poisoned marine life, and decimated the fishing and tourist industries throughout the oil-spattered Gulf Coast. President Barack Obama called it "the worst environmental disaster America has ever faced." Shocked Americans turned on their televisions to images of brown pelicans encrusted in crude and sludge-stained beaches contaminated by the massive runoff from the gushing well.

Many of the workers who survived the blast were apparently not so shocked. A month before the explosion happened, investigators from a risk-management firm called Lloyd's Register Group conducted a survey of safety conditions on the soon-to-be-infamous rig, the Deepwater Horizon, which was being leased by BP, a company with a checkered history on such matters. The investigators interviewed forty workers, some of whom told them that they "often saw unsafe behaviors" but were too scared to report them. "Only about half of the workers interviewed said they felt they could report actions leading to a potentially 'risky' situation without reprisal," reported *The New York Times* in a front-page story about the investigation.

It may not have been a wise career move for workers on the Deepwater Horizon to speak out about their concerns. Yet had more done so, vital warnings might have surfaced that could have spared the shrimpers, oyster harvesters, and beachgoers of the Gulf from untold anguish and distress, underscoring an irony noted by the legal scholar Cass Sunstein in his book *Why Societies Need Dissent*. "Conformists are often thought to be protective of social interests, keeping quiet for the sake of the group," observed Sunstein. "By contrast, dissenters tend to be seen as selfish individualists, embarking on projects of their own. But in an important sense, the opposite is closer to the truth. Much of the time, dissenters benefit others, while conformists benefit themselves."

One benefit dissenters bestow on society is to bring information to light that can prevent disastrous social blunders. Sunstein cited the example of the bungled Bay of Pigs invasion in 1961, when none of John F. Kennedy's senior advisers dared to say they thought the idea of launching a stealth attack on Cuba was misguided, as some of them apparently believed. "Had one senior advisor opposed the adventure, I believe that Kennedy would have canceled it," Arthur Schlesinger, Jr., who was among the advisers, later wrote. "In the months after the Bay of Pigs I bitterly reproached myself for having kept so silent during those crucial discussions."

It's a compelling anecdote, underscoring how much of a difference even one person who musters the courage to speak out can make. Yet its power hinges on the premise that Kennedy would have paid attention to the dissenting voice at the table. What if, instead, he'd nodded politely and gone right ahead with the plan? What if some workers on the Deepwater Horizon rig had overcome their misgivings and aired their concerns about safety conditions, perhaps even going so far as to organize a press conference or run a newspaper ad, and few people bothered to take their warnings seriously—or even to notice?

In dictatorships and police states, one of the few things individuals who voice dissent never have to fear is that nobody will pay attention to them. In his famous essay "The Power of the Powerless," the Czech dissident Václav Havel offered the example of an employee at a brewery ("a certain S") who had the temerity to write a critical letter to the authorities about the plant manager, who everyone knew was driving the establishment to ruin. The worker took the trouble to exercise voice, and his reward was to be labeled a "political saboteur" and shifted to a different plant where he would never be heard from again, a fairly predictable (and mild) rebuke in light of the fact that the manager of the brewery was a well-connected member of the Communist Party's district committee. "By speaking the truth, S had stepped out of line, broken the rules, cast himself out, and he ended up as a sub-citizen," wrote Havel.

In democracies, dissenting voices cannot be forcibly silenced this way—"living in truth" was not a crime. But they can be—and often are—ignored. Eight years before the scope of Bernard Madoff's Ponzi scheme was revealed to his clients and patrons, a financial analyst named Harry Markopolos began sending the SEC detailed reports showing that the amazing returns generated by Madoff Securities were mathematically impossible. Markopolos spoke up, repeatedly, meticulously documenting his claims, and the response ranged between yawns and silence. Markopolos also tried to tip off some reporters, with little more success. He later published an account of his futile effort to drum up interest in the largest Ponzi scheme in history, titled, appropriately, *No One Would Listen.*

This is how Leyla felt after the NASD arbitrators listened with stony passivity to her testimony—not silenced but ignored by people who heard her out but didn't seem to care—and when her letter to the SEC seemed to disappear into a void. She made slightly more headway on October 27, 2004, a month or so after the NASD had closed her case, when, out of desperation, she got hold of the number of an attorney at the examination branch of the SEC's Fort Worth District Office. Leyla dialed the number and relayed the details of her story to him, explaining that she'd been fired and was about to lose her license unless she paid more than $100,000 to a company she believed was committing massive fraud. An anonymous letter was one thing, a conversation with an actual regulator in the state where Stanford was based quite another, she figured. Two months later, in December, she got a call from Victoria Prescott, special senior counsel at the same branch of the SEC, to whom she repeated her story and then sent a FedEx package with the reports she'd gathered.

Months passed. Nothing happened. If anyone at the SEC shared her alarm about Stanford, they did an extremely good job of hiding it from her. Leyla did hear from one person—her lawyer, who told her that Stanford had contacted him to say it was open to a settlement. For a compromise sum—$50,000, he suggested—she could retain her license and move on. Pride battered, savings depleted, Leyla took out a loan and reluctantly wired over a check. Four years later, in January 2009, she finally did hear from the SEC, when an investigator called her cell phone. "He said, 'I want to talk to you about a prior employer,'" Leyla recalled. "I said, 'Let me guess who—Stanford?' He just laughed."

Leyla wasn't laughing. "I wanted to scream," she told me, "at everyone."

"A legal system that is committed to free speech forbids government from silencing dissenters," observed Cass Sunstein. "That is an extraordinary accomplishment." But as he went on to note, the legal right to free speech was not enough to guarantee that individuals who exercised it in situations that cried out for opposition actually had any impact. "Even in democracies, disparities in power play a large role in silencing dissent—sometimes by ensuring that dissenters keep quiet, but more insidiously by ensuring that dissenters are not really heard." A properly functioning democratic society, Sunstein argued, "has a culture of free speech" that "encourages a certain set of attitudes in listeners, one that gives a respectful hearing to those who do not embrace the conventional wisdom. In a culture of free speech, the attitude of listeners is no less important than that of speakers."

Of course, even in a well-functioning democracy, the quality of the listening varies depending on who is talking, which isn't necessarily a bad thing. Not every insider who contacts a federal agency convinced a nefarious plot is under way can be guaranteed a respectful hearing. Nor do all deserve one, since agencies have limited resources and since, for every conscientious whistleblower with a legitimate complaint, there are untold numbers of cranks and crackpots with specious ones. Sometimes people with suspicious minds are onto something important; other times they're a bit paranoid, unbalanced, or insane. In his book, C. Fred Alford described how even other whistleblowers didn't always find it easy to listen to the individuals who showed up at support groups to talk about their travails—a former government auditor named Mary, for example, who regaled her peers with stories pervaded by numerological coincidences ("Seven years after she was fired she lived on the seventh floor in an apartment with seven locks that was broken into"). Alford noted the conspiratorial undertone that often crept into whistleblowers' accounts of the ordeals they'd undergone:

"Nothing just follows, everything is causally connected, and the whistleblower is the prime mover."

I spent a week in Houston with Leyla, and at no point heard her voice any conspiracy theories. Suspicion bordering on paranoia was another matter. "I'm not going to lie to you," she told me about midway through my visit, "there are times when I thought, Oh my God, what if he is a spy?"

He, it appears, was me.

"It's a very sensitive thing I have here," she went on. "What if Allen Stanford has hired him to come and know everything about me—to kill me, I don't know. My whole family has been afraid of this whole Stanford situation because it's a powerful— he's been powerful. I'm talking really powerful. He's been to Washington. He's hired people from all over. He had an empire, and it's down, and this little person moved these things. And then there's the government, and God knows what's behind all this. And I have my thoughts about this—I think he had a lot of political connections."

The next day, Leyla and I had lunch at Teotihuacan, a Mexican restaurant a few blocks from her office. Leyla smoked a cigarette outside afterward, a habit she indulged on occasion when feeling stressed. Then we got on the Loop and drove to a place that explained why her nerves might have been on edge, Stanford's headquarters, which I'd told her I was curious to visit. Leyla hadn't been back since losing her job. When we neared the building, turning onto a side street where a guard stood watch by the entrance to the former parking lot, I unbuckled my seat belt to persuade him to let us inside, so we could see what had become of the elegant dining room and spacious office where Leyla had once entertained her clients. Leyla, looking pale and tense, had thought better of this idea, telling me she'd prefer to stay in the car. "Don't say you're with me," she added; "I'm the whistleblower."

Given that Allen Stanford occupied a cell at the Joe Corley detention facility in Conroe, Texas, awaiting trial by this point, the precaution was likely unnecessary. Yet if the mere sight of Stanford's headquarters spooked Leyla, if she still worried someone might be out to get her, she was not alone. The day after we visited the company's former headquarters together, I drove to an office park to meet Mark Tidwell and Charles Rawl, the Stanford brokers who resigned in 2007, five years after Leyla lost her job, and then filed a lawsuit against the firm alleging that they were forced out because they didn't want to engage in improprieties. Like Leyla, both passed along some of what they knew to the SEC, which by the time of their departure had launched an investigation into the sale of Stanford's CDs, and like her, they were also sued by Stanford, which demanded that they pay their bonuses back. After taking an elevator up a couple of flights, I was led into an air-conditioned conference room with a glass cabinet full of tropical fish sculptures, and spent several hours listening to Rawl and Tidwell describe how, after leaving Stanford, they began to fear for their lives.

"I'm a pretty tough guy, I can handle a lot," Tidwell, a square-shouldered, solidly built man with a neatly trimmed goatee and thick black hair streaked with silver, told me, "but this was a challenge." By this, he meant the letters that he and Rawl received just about every week warning them of various offenses, among them that the allegations in their lawsuit amounted to defamation of character. One arrived on his doorstep hours before his family Christmas party, said Rawl, a tall man with a boyish face, sandy blond hair, and slightly bulging blue eyes that quivered faintly as he dredged up the memory. There were no death threats in these letters, no veiled warnings that someone might be physically harmed, yet the combination of feeling that a billion-dollar company regarded them as "the enemy" and knowing that it likely had a great deal to hide left neither man terribly reassured. "You turn on a light and it doesn't come on, the first thing through your mind is the lightbulb burned out," said Tidwell. "No, that wasn't the first thing through our minds during that time." Driving home at night, both he and Rawl took to scanning their rearview mirrors with extra care. They slept no more than four or five hours a night. They had nightmares that Stanford would buy off the judge or arbitrators who would end up deciding their case, and deploy every weapon in its arsenal to ruin them. "*Steamrolled* is the analogy I would use," said Tidwell. "They were going to Mack-truck us, steamroll us, we were going to be obliterated."

I left Rawl and Tidwell's office wondering whether, in some ways, it was harder—more socially isolating, more psychologically disorienting—to feel that someone was out to obliterate you in a prosperous, peaceful city like Houston than in, say, war-blasted Vukovar. I also wondered what I would have made of their story if they'd told me about the sinister machinations being plotted against them a year earlier, in 2008, when Stanford still possessed a sterling reputation among a lot of brokers in Houston. Most likely, I'd have taken them for a pair of disgruntled employees given to conspiratorial fantasies. Or reached the conclusion their coworkers and Rawl's wife drew, which is that they were crazy.

Near the end of our meeting, I asked them what kept them from going crazy. Rawl leaned forward and said, "Faith had a large part in it. I'm a more faithful person today than when I started." Then he glanced at Tidwell and said, "Without friendship, partnership, and faith, I wouldn't be sitting here today." In fact, both he and Tidwell lost a lot of their friends after leaving Stanford. But the experience evidently deepened their bond, and illustrated what both Stanley Milgram and Solomon Asch discovered in the experiments they conducted: that breaking ranks is significantly easier when a person can draw on some form of "mutual support," when there is another person who sees things the way you do.

Leyla drew this support from somewhere else—not a coworker but William, the man with whom she got together to go over Stanford's financial statements back when her troubles began. They continued seeing each other after she lost her job, and eventually a romance bloomed. By the time I met Leyla, she and William were married. They were also business partners: he occupied an office one floor down from hers at Casa Milagro, the real estate company they'd started together. A quiet, balding man with soft features and an avuncular manner, William minimized the role he played in her story—she blew the whistle because she cared deeply about her clients, he insisted, not because of anything he said—but did not understate the emotional toll the experience took on her. "Her pride was stepped on," he told me. "There was a question mark in the minds of other people who respected her but thought maybe she was not that knowledgeable about what she was saying. Some people thought she was a liar."

Leyla drew comfort from two other people, her daughter, Adriana, and her son, Armando, a quick-witted twenty-four-year-old who dropped by her office one day. "I remember when she signed with Stanford," Armando told me. "You know, it was a huge thing, it was like a blessing. It seemed like we were gonna be set—great bonus, college can be paid for, debts can be paid off, mortgage on the house." The period that followed, when she started feeling pressure from management to sell CDs, was turbulent, as much because of what Armando sensed was going on inside his mother's mind as because of anything she said. "This was definitely a man-versus-self"—he corrected himself—"a woman-versus-self conflict. She was definitely conflicted about it, you could just see it. She didn't want to lose her job, but she also didn't wanna be the black sheep, you know what I'm saying?" I asked Armando if he remembered the day she got fired. He nodded. "It was devastating, devastating," he said. "It was like a slap in the face, and then it was—shit, what are we gonna do now? Legal battles, the fight to keep her money, she had to hire a lawyer, I thought we were gonna go bankrupt. It was definitely a scary time."

Armando said he was too young to understand what exactly Stanford had done that was so wrong. I asked him if, in light of this, he ever thought his mother might have misjudged the situation. He shook his head emphatically. "No," he said. "Not once." Then I asked him if, now that he was older, he'd ever given thought to what he would have done in her shoes. He stroked his chin and gazed at his sneakers. "Good question, good question," he said, blinking his pale eyes. "I don't know. I might have done it for a while. Just because I can see how it would be very tough for somebody to thumb their nose at this eight-billion-dollar man. And to have two kids and all these expenses and to lose your job. If I had another job at that point, maybe, but my job, my bonus . . ." His voice trailed off.

"My mom would hate me for that, by the way," he added, a fear I suspected was misplaced, since what he'd said merely reflected the conflicted feelings her travails unsurprisingly stirred in him. Armando clearly admired his mother—she was "the strongest person I know," he told me. But he also clearly felt the burden of living up to her example, and had seen the price that standing by her principles exacted. Maybe he doubted sometimes whether he was strong enough to pay this price himself. Or just wished she'd been a bit less principled, sparing herself, and him, from the turmoil that engulfed their lives just when it seemed they'd made it.

"Do I wish my mother would have stayed there and continued to make money?" Armando asked me suddenly, as though reading my mind. "Kind of, you know."

There were lots of other people in Houston who likely felt the same way, albeit for different reasons. To judge by *Time*'s cover story back in 2002, whistleblowers were harassed and vilified until proven right, at which point they morphed into folk heroes. In reality, being right not infrequently made things worse. For if the person who blew the whistle was justified, what did this say about all the people who didn't? About the team players who'd profited handsomely by remaining silent? "That's part of the reason why so many of those other advisers hate us," Charlie Rawl had told me. "They were at a lot of the same meetings we were at. We're symbols of what they should have done."

Being such a symbol is what led Leyla to receive a standing ovation after she spoke at the Senate Banking Committee hearing on Stanford in Baton Rouge—and what caused her to agonize over whether to go there and testify. "I don't know if my husband told you," she said the morning after we visited Stanford's headquarters, my last day in Houston, "but I could not eat, I was hyperventilating for the whole week before I testified. I was a nervous wreck, in my stomach, in my body, it was like this whole thing pulling and pulling and pulling"—she clenched her fists into two tight balls—"constantly, twenty-four hours."

The source of Leyla's unease was no longer that people from the Financial Industry Regulatory Authority (FINRA)—to which the NASD had changed its name by this point—or the SEC might not listen to what she had to say. It was that they'd be listening with great attentiveness, and resenting her for embarrassing them. Leyla was still a registered financial adviser when she fielded the invitation to testify, having secured a position with a small independent broker-dealer. A month before the hearing was scheduled to take place, in July 2009, she'd spoken publicly about her experience at Stanford for the first time, in an interview with Adam Shapiro of Fox News. Not long after it aired, a manager at her broker-dealer called her to say he had watched the segment and was terminating her. "He said, 'You badmouthed the regulators,'" Leyla recalled. The manager was also upset about an anonymous letter that FINRA had received and apparently forwarded, indicating that Leyla had established a recovery group for Stanford's victims and could potentially be earning money from this.

Leyla was flabbergasted: the same agency that had ignored the anonymous letter she'd sent about Stanford's Ponzi scheme years earlier was now taking action about a potential ethical violation by her, because she'd taken the initiative to help victims of the crime recover some of their losses. "That's when I really felt like saying, This is it," Leyla told me. "I don't want to be in this industry anymore—it makes me so sick." As after the Enron scandal, Leyla thought about switching careers. And, as back then, she decided instead to use her voice, calling the head of her firm to explain what had happened and mentioning how it would look if Fox News aired a follow-up segment about how the Stanford whistleblower the network had just interviewed had been fired by another company for speaking out. The broker-dealer quickly reversed course and raised no objections when Leyla's lawyer subsequently informed the company that she was planning to attend the Senate Banking Committee hearing.

And yet, for all of this, Leyla still felt deeply torn about testifying, not because it might get her into trouble but because of the sense of loyalty she still harbored for an industry that had disappointed her at every turn. "Being in front of the regulators, being in front of a senator, I'd never been exposed to any of that," she told me. "And I was a registered financial adviser. I felt that I am—like I'm betraying my industry, telling on my industry, on an industry that I loved so much, for such a long time."

The hearing in Baton Rouge was called by the Republican senator David Vitter of Louisiana, who, with his colleague Richard Shelby of Alabama, would go on to compose a letter to the SEC's Office of Inspector General (OIG) requesting a "comprehensive and complete investigation" of the agency's handling of the Stanford matter. It was the least the angry senators could do for the downcast investors who lived in their respective states, though, notably, it was not accompanied by calls to investigate another institution whose dealings with the firm merited scrutiny: the one they served in. Not everyone could get a respectful hearing in a democracy, but if you disbursed $2.3 million to politicians and spent an additional $5 million lobbying Congress, as Stanford did between 1999 and

2008, it turned out your chances were pretty good. Stanford lavished particular attention on members of the Caribbean Caucus, a group of congressional representatives who were flown out to Antigua on its private jets, put up in luxury hotels, and treated to lobster and caviar dinners while touring the island and hobnobbing with Allen Stanford. "If it wasn't for Allen, I certainly would not be here today," the New York congressman John Sweeney, a member of the caucus, told *The Antigua Sun* during one such excursion. "People take notice of a man of his standing and stature in the halls of Washington." Notice him they did. In 2001, Stanford paid $100,000 to a national lobbying group that sought to quash a bill before the Senate Banking Committee that would have allowed state and federal regulators to exchange information about fraud investigations. The bill never came up for a vote. A year earlier, a bill that would have increased federal regulation of offshore bankers materialized. Stanford dispensed $40,000 to the Senate Republican Campaign Committee and $100,000 to the inaugural committee of George W. Bush. (To cover its bases, the company lavished an additional $500,000 on Democrats.) The measure died quietly.

"I love you and believe in you," Congressman Pete Sessions, chairman of the National Republican Congressional Committee and a recipient of $44,375 in campaign donations from Stanford and his staff, wrote to Allen Stanford in an e-mail on February 17, 2009, hours after federal agents descended on the company's headquarters.

The investigation requested by Senators Vitter and Shelby did not look into whether Stanford might have bought off and silenced their colleagues. It was restricted to the SEC, and it was released to the press on April 16, 2010, the same day the agency filed a civil suit against Goldman Sachs, charging the firm with fraudulently marketing a collateralized debt obligation (CDO) tied to subprime mortgages. The timing worked out splendidly for the SEC, with the Goldman suit dominating the headlines and the OIG's scathing exposé of its glaring misconduct barely noticed. The first SEC investigation of Stanford took place in 1997, the OIG found, three years before Leyla began working at the company, when the examination group of the SEC's Fort Worth office performed a review. The eye-popping returns of Stanford's CDs were "absolutely ludicrous," the branch chief determined at the time. "Possible misrepresentations. Possible Ponzi scheme," the investigation concluded. The enforcement group of the SEC's Fort Worth office responded to this alarming information with a three-month investigation that was abruptly terminated, during which its only action was a voluntary request for documents from Stanford, which the company refused. Four years later came another report by the examination group. Once again the above-market returns of Stanford's CDs were deemed potentially fraudulent; once again nothing was done. A third examination-group report was completed in 2002, and soon thereafter the agency began to hear from some concerned outsiders, including an accountant in Mexico whose seventy-five-year-old mother had all her savings invested in Stanford's CDs. "Please review very well Stanford to make sure that many investors do not get cheated," the accountant wrote to the SEC on October 28, 2002. "These investors are simple people . . . and have their faith in the United States financial system."

"This is great, we've actually got somebody complaining," one examiner at the SEC exulted, drafting a reply explaining that with her permission the agency could forward her letter to Stanford and ask the company to explain why the CDs were a suitable investment for an elderly woman in Mexico. "That response might be enlightening to all of us," the examiner's note stated, and indeed it might have been, except that no such request was sent, with the SEC's enforcement division bizarrely deciding to forward the letter from the Mexican accountant to the Texas State Securities Board instead, a state agency that didn't deal with such matters. What did the regulators there do with the letter? Apparently nothing, since the OIG was unable to find any record of it being received.

Leyla's letter wasn't similarly mishandled, and was actually discussed by various people at the SEC who deemed her concern a "tire kicker"—that is, not a priority. "Rather than spend a lot of resources on something that could end up being something that we could not bring, the decision was made to—to not go forward at that time, or at least to—to not spend the significant resources and—and wait and see if something else would come up," a member of the enforcement unit explained. As the OIG report noted of this jaw-dropping statement,

> It is not clear what the Enforcement staff hoped to gain by "wait[ing] [to] see if something else would come up" after the SEC had conducted three examinations of SGC [Stanford Group Company] finding that the SIB CDs were probably a Ponzi scheme; received a letter from a relative of an investor concerned about the legitimacy of those CDs ... and received an anonymous letter from a Stanford insider telling the SEC that Stanford was operating a "massive Ponzi scheme."

One excuse for the SEC's inaction was jurisdictional, with Leyla's letter prompting discussion about whether there were any U.S. investors involved (there were) and whether the agency could get access to foreign records pertaining to Stanford International Bank. Yet this hardly explained why a broker-dealer based in Texas that the SEC's own investigators believed was violating numerous domestic securities laws, including Section 206 of the Investment Advisers Act, which obligated the firm's advisers to perform due diligence about Stanford's investment portfolio, was left alone. The real reason no action was taken was the preference inside the agency for "quick hit" cases that wouldn't take much time, the OIG concluded, compounded by an apparent desire to remain on chummy terms with a powerful company in the industry that the SEC was supposed to be policing. The assistant director of the Fort Worth enforcement branch who repeatedly refrained from ordering any injunctive action was a man named Spencer Barasch. After he left the SEC, Barasch sought to represent Stanford on three occasions and actually did so, briefly, in 2006.

At one point while in Houston, I spoke on the phone to a man named Luis, the proprietor of a family-run tire company in Mexico who'd been a client of Leyla's before she started working at Stanford and still entrusted her to manage his money. When Leyla was fired from Stanford, Luis spoke to her about the CDs; he listened to her warnings and decided to keep two-thirds of his assets invested in them anyway. I asked him why. "They sounded professional," he said. "They were saying it was a bank growing rapidly, that it was getting better numbers and better numbers—it wins your confidence." Leyla's warnings, he added, were "hard to believe," and one of the reasons was the overweening confidence Luis had in the U.S. financial system. "Before, you felt that the institutions were working better in America than in other countries and that those institutions were guarded by government entities, ratings agencies," he told me. "It gave you a sense of security, that there were locks on the system." And now? "Now I feel they are crooked and take advantage of people any way they can."

I wondered often how Leyla had avoided undergoing similar disillusionment, and gradually came to realize that actually she hadn't. "I really thought that Wall Street was being honest, was good," she told me. "The regulators were regulating. Government was doing its job, okay. I never thought that these things that I've seen in the last ten years would happen. I had so much confidence in our system. I really did." She smiled. "I don't anymore." There was something else I wondered about, which is whether, after reading the OIG report, after seeing that everything she'd undergone—getting fired, feeling betrayed, fearing for her life—had been met with little more than a bureaucratic shrug, she would do the same thing again. I asked Leyla this question over the phone. There was a long pause.

"Probably so," she said finally. "Yeah, I would. I would have done it again, because"—she paused again—"it was the right thing to do.

"It's just," she continued, searching for the words, "I don't know, it's a need. It was the right thing to do, and I feel like my actions, my intentions, have to have a sort of meaning in this life."

The halting voice, the long silences, suggested this was one question Leyla preferred not to dwell on. Perhaps thinking about it was too dispiriting. Or perhaps privately she entertained some doubts about whether going through life so firmly anchored to one's convictions was really worth it, as Armando did. Yet the more I got to know Leyla, the more I sensed that she didn't draw her greatest satisfaction from things that came easily to her. She drew it from the process of overcoming the unexpected obstacles that always seemed to be falling in her path. So it was when she'd been an unemployed single mother with two toddlers, no money, and breast cancer. And so it was in Baton Rouge, where, looking out at the sea of former Stanford investors in the audience, many of them senior citizens with gray hair and walking canes, Leyla felt a pang of outrage. She also felt the fury of the regulators on hand, including a man from FINRA who fixed her with a contemptuous glare. "He looked at me, in my eyes, like, Why are you doing that?" she recalled. "You're betraying us. How dare you. That's what he was telling me with his eyes." Then she started speaking and, as often in the past when facing her biggest fears, her nerves steadied, and she found her courage. "When I was sitting reading it, that's when my fear went away," she told me. "It was like a light came into me. My voice grew and I said it very clearly. Everything just felt perfect, perfect."

EPILOGUE

The journey that I embarked on after visiting the forest in Józefów ended by a lake in Erie, Pennsylvania, where I drove to see Darrel Vandeveld. We met on a clear, mild day in March, nearly four years after Vandeveld started working as a senior prosecutor at the Office of Military Commissions, in Guantánamo. He arrived there on the heels of a thirteen-month tour of duty in Iraq, where he earned a Bronze Star while serving in a unit that suffered heavy casualties from roadside bombs and insurgent attacks. The bonds among the men in the unit were extremely intense, Vandeveld told me, which fueled his determination to bring as many enemy combatants to justice as possible. "I believed the detainees held at Guantánamo were the worst of the worst—the baddest, most evil men, bent on the destruction not just of the United States but of Western civilization," he said. "My mission was to avenge, if I could, those comrades I had lost in battle."

Vandeveld was soon handling one of every three Guantánamo prosecutions. Among them was *United States v. Mohammed Jawad*. Jawad was an Afghan detainee accused of hurling a grenade that hit a U.S. Army vehicle at a crowded bazaar in Kabul on December 17, 2002, seriously wounding two Special Forces soldiers and an interpreter. The crime struck a chord in Vandeveld, who had developed immense respect for members of the Special Forces while in Iraq, and who, after reviewing the evidence, told me he viewed it as "a perfect case"—easy to prove and bereft of moral ambiguity. At a pretrial hearing, when Jawad recited a litany of complaints about mistreatment he'd endured at the hands of his U.S. captors, Vandeveld rolled his eyes and ridiculed the claim, telling the military judge that the defendant had "taken a page out of the al-Qaeda handbook" by inventing specious charges of abuse.

He hadn't yet examined Jawad's prison logs, which came to his attention after David Frakt, an officer in the U.S. Air Force Reserve who took over as his defense attorney midway through the case, filed a motion to see them. During one two-week period at Guantánamo, the logs showed, Jawad had been moved from cell to cell 112 times, a regimen known as the "frequent flyer program" that was used to deprive detainees of sleep. Some time later, Vandeveld spotted a document in a binder in a colleague's bookcase in which an Army Criminal Investigation Division special agent described a prisoner being hooded, shackled, thrown down a staircase, and slapped by U.S. interrogators in Afghanistan. The prisoner was Mohammed Jawad. The complaint had not been made available to Jawad's attorney, nor had a government report about another suspect who had confessed to the grenade attack for which Jawad was being tried. Vandeveld soon came across newspaper stories indicating that, on the day of the attack, three other suspects in the vicinity had been arrested. All three had been released after paying off the Afghan police. At the time of his arrest, it turned out Jawad was likely no older than sixteen, which meant that under the Geneva Conventions he should have been treated as a child soldier, with a focus on rehabilitation rather than punishment.

Seeking a way to reconcile his duties as a prosecutor with his growing doubts about the case, Vandeveld recommended that a plea deal be arranged, in which Jawad would agree to serve another year and then be released. After his superiors dismissed this idea, he made his way to a monastery in Washington, D.C. A devout Catholic, he told me he spent three days immersed in prayer, and left having decided he could no longer continue doing his job. Soon after informing the army of this, he was subpoenaed to testify in Mohammed Jawad's trial—by David Frakt, the defense attorney. In court, Vandeveld methodically detailed the steps that had slowly led him to doubt the validity of the government's charges. "Mr. Jawad's continued detention is unsupported by any credible evidence, any provision of the Detainee Treatment Act of 2005 . . . international law or our own hallowed Constitution," he stated. A judge subsequently ruled that Jawad's self-incriminating statements had been extracted under torture and, after Jawad had spent nearly seven years in prison, ordered him to be released.

It is "our moral duty to confront evil in all its forms," George W. Bush stated at a ceremony honoring Paul Rusesabagina for the courage he'd displayed in Rwanda in 1994. But as Darrel Vandeveld learned, fulfilling this duty is almost never welcome when it proves embarrassing to your government. After he informed his superiors of his ethical qualms, the army ordered him to undergo a psychological evaluation. Instead of being reassigned to Afghanistan or Iraq, as he requested, Vandeveld was released from active duty and made to feel like a traitor who, despite two Joint Meritorious Unit Awards and a Bronze Star, had disgraced his country, with Lawrence Morris, the chief prosecutor at Guantánamo, telling the press there were "no grounds" for his misgivings. Compared with what some people who refuse to compromise their principles undergo, this was a minor punishment, but that did not make it pleasant. "To be attacked for your deeply held beliefs that you've thought through and agonized over—that was a very difficult thing," Vandeveld told me. "This personal assault on what I pride myself on most—my devotion to duty, my desire to do the right thing—I had no experience or tools to be able to contextualize that."

Why would anyone put himself through such an ordeal? Was it worth it? During the course of my travels, as I listened to individuals who refused to relax their principles talk about the travails they'd endured, I often found myself doubting this, particularly when so little seemed to have changed. Darrel Vandeveld had clearly entertained similar doubts. Nearly three years after his dismissal, the detention center in Guantánamo was still up and running, while his life had been upended. He had recently been invited to speak at an event at Harvard Law School titled "The Razor's Edge: Standing on Principle/Risking Your Career," where a political scientist who'd written a book about dissent made an observation that resonated with him. "He said the idea that an individual dissenter can have an effect is mistaken," Vandeveld told me. "Reluctantly, I've come to the same conclusion. You don't bring about change. You only bring pain on yourself."

It was an honest statement, born of experience, and it made me wonder what the law students in attendance had taken away from the event—a lesson on how not to derail their careers? On why they should scrupulously avoid drifting near "the razor's edge"? Reporters like to imagine that stories of moral courage will inspire people as the uplifting tales of principled defiance cause the spirit of resistance to spread. But if the stories are told honestly and accurately, isn't it just as likely the opposite will happen: that instead of growing, the ranks of those willing to risk their careers and stand on principle will dwindle?

Darrel Vandeveld seemed to suggest as much. And yet when I asked him if he regretted what he'd done, he shook his head. "I'd be less than human if I were to deny that I regret some of the consequences that followed from it," he said, "but the basic decision? No, I don't." One reason, it turned out, was that Vandeveld was not, in fact, an "individual dissenter." He was one of seven officials at Guantánamo who'd stepped down, complained, or resigned after experiencing similar ethical qualms. The first, a U.S. Army

Reserve officer named Stephen Abraham, ended up filing an affidavit in the case of *Boumediene v. Bush*, which came before the Supreme Court and which led to detainees at Guantánamo being granted habeas corpus rights. Since Mohammed Jawad's trial, some other things had changed for the better, Vandeveld told me, which he attributed not only to the collective impact of the officials who'd spoken out but also to outside pressure groups that echoed their complaints. "The commissions as they exist today are much fairer than they were at the start. They place limits on the use of coerced testimony, they afford the accused many more rights, and they redefine some of the crimes," he said. "It would be foolish of me to claim credit for that, but it was the product of not only my dissent within the commissions but also those of civil rights groups, the ACLU, the Center for Constitutional Rights—they all had an effect."

They had an effect because, even when the people engaging in them have more limited ambitions, acts of conscience have a way of reverberating. Who knows whether the first soldier in Israel who refused to serve in the occupied territories wanted to do anything more than keep his own hands clean, but the fact is that in the decades since, hundreds of other conscripts have done the same thing. It surely wasn't Paul Grüninger's aim to prompt Switzerland to reexamine its past and engage in some collective soul-searching when he disobeyed the law in 1938, but that is what his singular act of principled noncooperation played a role in doing. It wasn't Thoreau's ambition "to devote himself to the eradication of any, even the most enormous wrong," he insisted, but the essay he wrote about why he wouldn't pay a poll tax ended up inspiring some conscientious objectors to do just that, among them Martin Luther King, Jr., who read it as a student and was deeply influenced by Thoreau's words. ("I became convinced that noncooperation with evil is as much a moral obligation as is cooperation with good," wrote King in his autobiography. "No other person has been more eloquent and passionate in getting this idea across than

Henry David Thoreau. As a result of his writings and personal witness, we are the heirs of a legacy of creative protest.")

Why do such ripple effects occur when, as courts have sometimes ruled, conscience is "a merely personal moral code," the faculty that individuals consult when disregarding other voices? In part because, as the philosopher Michael Walzer has persuasively argued, this isn't exactly true. The word *conscience* implies "a shared knowledge of good and evil," a set of precepts that take shape not in isolation but through interaction with other citizens and engagement in groups, sects, political parties, labor unions, professional organizations, military units. "There is a difference between personal decisions and the moral code on which such decisions are based," Walzer observes. "The decisions we may finally make alone; the code we almost certainly share."

In every society, there are rebels and iconoclasts who don't share the moral code to which most of their fellow citizens subscribe—who delight in thumbing their noses at whatever authority figure will pay them mind. The resisters featured in these pages are not among them. Their problem was not that they airily dismissed the values and ideals of the societies they lived in or the organizations they belonged to, but that they regarded them as inviolable. For Paul Grüninger, the inviolable ideal was the tradition of welcoming strangers he thought all Swiss citizens cherished as much as he did. For Aleksander Jevtić, it was the spirit of tolerance passed along by his mother and embodied in the slogan "Brotherhood and Unity." For Avner Wishnitzer, it was a belief that the Israeli army really was "the most moral army in the world," and for Leyla Wydler, it was the responsibility to exercise the due diligence she thought all members of her profession were obligated to practice. They were naïve to believe these things, a cynic with a more jaded outlook might aver. But had they been more cynical or jaded, they would not have felt so committed to the principles they assumed should be guiding them, or so disillusioned when they saw them being compromised and ignored.

"I went from being a true believer to someone who felt truly deceived," Darrel Vandeveld told me. As with the other nonconformists I met, it was his investment in the ideals he saw being tarnished that led him to act—and, no less important, his willingness to exercise his moral imagination in ways that got in the way of doing his job. This capacity is universal, argued Adam Smith, and he was right: it doesn't take special hardwiring or saintly virtue to feel sympathy for the people we might be harming by falling silent or going along. But no less universal is the tendency to shut the moral imagination off—by distancing ourselves from the consequences of our actions, by justifying them on the basis of an ideology, by shifting responsibility for the harm we may be causing to someone above or below us in the chain of command. In a world governed by large, impersonal forces, where the link between cause and effect is increasingly unclear, individuals thrust into compromising situations are rarely at a loss for opportunities to disavow responsibility in this way, not only when the dilemmas are extreme but, perhaps even more so, when they are prosaic. It's easy enough to judge soldiers at Abu Ghraib or bystanders during World War II who failed to find their courage when unconscionable things were happening before their eyes. It's a lot harder to acknowledge or even realize how often we avoid making uncomfortable choices in the course of our daily lives by attributing the small injustices that momentarily grate at our consciences to the system, or the circumstances, or our superiors. Or how rarely we bother to ask what role our own passivity and acquiescence may play in enabling unconscionable things to be done in our name.

To judge by the sanctimonious tributes made to those who "confront evil" in places like Rwanda or by *Time* magazine's tribute to whistleblowers who spoke out about accounting fraud in the United States, we live in a world where overcoming passivity and acquiescence is seen as honorable. In reality, we all know that doing so is risky and dangerous, not least because there is precious little agreement about where the line between duty and conscience should be drawn. Around torture, which much of the world officially banned centuries ago? Not according to those who vilified the handful of dissenters who challenged the abusive interrogation policies that were institutionalized during the Bush era. Around concocting clever ways to defraud people of their savings? Not according to the traders on Wall Street who did exactly that and profited, without pausing to apologize, during the period that preceded the 2008 financial crash (and who were not asked to apologize by politicians who proceeded to weaken or scuttle efforts to regulate their industry afterward). What about stealing people's land? Not according to Jewish settlers in the West Bank, who see this as a fulfillment of God's plan. Even people who do regard these things as unconscionable might find it unnerving to see a soldier, a public official, or a colleague at work take an uncompromising stand on the matter. For if we agree that something blatantly wrong is happening, shouldn't we be taking a similar stand? Do we really want to be reminded of the compromises we've made?

Inevitably, then, displays of moral courage sow discord and make a lot of people uncomfortable—most of all, perhaps, the true believer who never wanted or expected to say no. It is never easy to incur the wrath of an offended majority, to "fall out of step with one's tribe," observed Susan Sontag. And it's true: no one finds this painless. But it's considerably harder for insiders who've spent their lives fiercely identifying with the values of the majority than for dissenters accustomed to being on the margins, with their like-minded comrades by their side. Darrel Vandeveld's biggest fear was not losing his job, he told me, but betraying the soldiers who had fought, and sometimes died, for the values he went to Guantá-namo determined to uphold and defend. "The greatest source of internal conflict that I had was whether I was in some sense breaking faith with my comrades—particularly those who had been killed," he said. "Was I letting them down? Was I, in the worst sense, siding with the enemy?"

As it turns out, this fear was misplaced. To Vandeveld's great relief, not a single soldier in his unit ended up questioning his loyalty. "Darrel, we don't know what this is about, but we know you—call me if you need anything," he told me many of them wrote to him. "They knew me, and a bond is built up that will never be broken." Yet even if these bonds had frayed, I sensed Vandeveld still would not have regretted what he'd done, because he had managed to avoid betraying the one person whose judgment he knew he would not be able to evade: his own. Newspapers that published accounts of his story inevitably drew attention to the reprisals he faced from the army, as I have here. They did not mention the unquantifiable thing he'd gained, something that explained the hint of gratitude that occasionally crept into his voice as he talked about his experience and that some of his former colleagues might have found enviable. "I went to Guantánamo on a mission," he told me, "and the mission that I achieved was perhaps my own salvation."

NOTES

PROLOGUE

4 For a description of the massacre at Józefów see Christopher Browning, *Ordinary Men* (HarperCollins, 1992), chapters 1 and 7.

6 *"our moral duty"*: George W. Bush, "Citations for Recipients of the 2005 Presidential Medal of Freedom," accessed May 11, 2011, georgewbush -whitehouse.archives.gov/news/releases/2005/11/20051109-10.html.

6 For Darby's story and aftermath see Anderson Cooper, "The Abu Ghraib Whistleblower," *60 Minutes*, June 25, 2007, accessed May 11, 2011, www .cbsnews.com/video/watch/?id=2972689n&tag=related;photovideo.

7 *"If someone had"*: S. Yizhar, *Khirbet Khizeh*, trans. Nicholas de Lange and Yaacob Dweck (Ibis Editions, 2008), p. 82.

9 *"terrifyingly normal"*: Hannah Arendt, *Eichmann in Jerusalem: A Report on the Banality of Evil* (Penguin, 1994), p. 276.

10 *"cannot be absolved"*: Browning, *Ordinary Men*, p. 188.

1. DISOBEYING THE LAW

11 For an account of Kristallnacht in Vienna see Martin Gilbert, *Kristallnacht: Prelude to Destruction* (HarperCollins, 2006), and U.S. Holocaust Memorial Museum website, "Vienna," accessed May 5, 2011, www.ushmm.org/wlc/ en/article.php?ModuleId=10005452.

12 For a brief description of the Evian Conference see Ronnie S. Landau, *The Nazi Holocaust* (Ivan R. Dee, 1994), pp. 137–40, and U.S. Holocaust

Memorial Museum website, "The Evian Conference," accessed May 11, 2011, www.ushmm.org/outreach/en/article.php?ModuleId=10007698.

12 For Swiss visa requirements leading up to World War II see Stefan Keller, *Délit d'humanité: l'affaire Grüninger* (D'en bas, 1994).

13 *"The asylum tradition"*: Independent Commission of Experts, *Switzerland and Refugees in the Nazi Era* (Bern, 1999), p. 45.

13 *"If we do not"*: Richard Dindo, dir., *Grüninger's Fall* (film), 0:09.

14 *"looking Jewish"*: Keller, *Délit*.

14 *"Can't we"*: *Switzerland and Refugees*, p. 66. For description of *J* stamp see p. 80.

14 *"without exception"*: Keller, *Délit*, p. 51.

15 For information on Grüninger's early life see Keller, *Délit*.

17 *"Sir, you no longer"*: ibid., p. 13.

17 *"special permission"*: ibid., p. 164.

17 *"Such underhanded practices"*: *Grüninger's Fall*, 1:24.

18 *"In my eyes"*: *Grüninger's Fall*, 1:07.

18 *"You are . . . in Europe"*: Mordecai Paldiel, *Diplomat Heroes of the Holocaust* (Ktav, 2007), pp. xi-xii.

20 For Mendes's story see *Diplomat Heroes*, pp. 71–88.

22 *"too open"*: Keller, *Délit*, p. 121.

23 *"ambiguous financial situation"*: *Grüninger's Fall*, 1:17.

23 *"men in uniforms"*: Zygmunt Bauman, *Modernity and the Holocaust* (Cornell, 1989), p. 151.

24 *"Cruelty correlates"*: ibid., p. 166.

24 For a description of the original Milgram experiment see Stanley Milgram, *Obedience to Authority* (Harper and Row, 1974), pp. 13–26.

25 *"He's in . . . go on"*: ibid., pp. 73–77.

25 *"agentic state . . . contribute"*: ibid., pp. 121, 133.

25 *"unpinnable"*: Bauman, *Modernity*, p. 163.

26 *"spared [them] . . . its victims"*: ibid., pp. 155–56.

26 For quotes and descriptions of Milgram's experiments with proximity see Milgram, *Obedience*, pp. 33–38.

27 *"Milgram's . . . did not"*: Eva Fogelman, *Conscience and Courage* (Doubleday, 1994), p. xiv.

27 For a description of the incident and Perlasca's response see ibid., pp. 52–55.

27 *"transforming encounter . . . events"*: ibid., pp. 52–54.

28 *"The approximately . . . long term"*: *Diplomat Heroes*, p. 83.

28 *"Whoever had the"*: *Grüninger's Fall*, 1:05.

29 *"I thought about"*: *Diplomat Heroes*, p. 124.

29 *"Studies designed to"*: Gilbert Harman, "Moral Philosophy Meets Social

Psychology: Virtue Ethics and the Fundamental Attribution Error," *Proceedings of the Aristotelian Society*, 1999, pp. 315–31.

30 *"the diffusion of responsibility"*: Bibb Latané and John Darley, *The Unresponsive Bystander: Why Doesn't He Help?* (Meredith, 1970), pp. 93–101.

30 *"As soon as"*: *Diplomat Heroes*, p. 124.

30 *"There were children"*: David Cesarani, *Becoming Eichmann* (Da Capo, 2004), p. 106.

31 *"Jew hunts . . . less clean"*: Browning, *Ordinary Men*, pp. 152, 175–76, 184. For critique of Goldhagen's theory see pp. 191–223. For "Jew hunts" see chapter 14.

32 *"The average"*: S.L.A. Marshall, *Men Against Fire: The Problem of Battle Command* (William Morrow, 1947), p. 79.

32 For the changes in U.S. army training see Dave Grossman, *On Killing: The Psychological Cost of Learning to Kill in War and Society* (Back Bay, 1995), pp. 160–64; for firing rate see p. 35; for quoted terms see pp. 73 and 146.

32 *"Border guards"*: *Diplomat Heroes*, p. 137.

34 *"Cheer up"*: *Grüninger's Fall*, 0:42.

35 *"We have ascertained"*: Keller, *Délit*, p. 82.

36 *"surprising proportions"*: ibid.

36 *"The mutual support"*: Milgram, *Obedience*, p. 121.

38 *"It would be"*: Keller, *Délit*.

39 *"humane actions"*: ibid. Quotations from the documents provided to me by Erich Billig.

42 *"gratitude and respect"*: ibid., pp. 219–20.

44 *"small, modest actions"*: François Rochat and Andre Modigliani, *The Ordinary Quality of Resistance: From Milgram's Laboratory to the Village of Le Chambon* (The Society of the Psychological Study of Social Issues, 1995), p. 197. Rochat and Modigliani apply this theory directly to Grüninger in "Captain Paul Grüninger," in the book *Obedience to Authority* (Lawrence Erlbaum Associates, 2000), edited by Thomas Blass.

44 *"It is obvious"*: *Diplomat Heroes*, p. 82.

2. DEFYING THE GROUP

47 For a description of the siege of Vukovar see Laura Silber and Allan Little, *Yugoslavia: Death of a Nation* (Penguin, 1997), pp. 175–82.

52 *"You may feel"*: Slavenka Drakulić, *The Balkan Express: Fragments from the Other Side of War* (Norton, 1993), p. 52.

52 *"the homogenization . . . against us"*: Misha Glenny, *The Fall of Yugoslavia* (Penguin, 1992), pp. 85–86.

57 For the scene of debris in the museum see Michael Ignatieff, *Blood and Belonging: Journeys into the New Nationalism* (Noonday, 1995), pp. 31–35.

59 *"is a . . . prejudice"*: Gordon W. Allport, *The Nature of Prejudice: 25th Anniversary Edition* (Perseus, 1979), pp. xv, xvii.

60 *"Get out . . . prison camps?"*: Peter Maass, *Love Thy Neighbor: A Story of War* (Vintage, 1996), pp. 20–21.

61 *"safe area . . . be killed"*: Matthew Lippman, "Humanitarian Law: The Development and Scope of the Superior Orders," *Penn State International Law Review*, Fall 2011, pp. 233–44.

63 *"Have courage"*: Immanuel Kant, *Foundations of the Metaphysics of Morals*, 2nd ed., trans. Lewis White Beck (Prentice Hall, 1989), p. 83.

63 *"Affective forces are"*: Quoted in Jonathan Haidt, "The Emotional Dog and Its Rational Tail," *Psychological Review*, vol. 108, no. 4, October 2001, p. 816. For more on Kohlberg's theory see Charles Bailey, "Kohlberg on Morality and Feeling," in *Lawrence Kohlberg: Consensus and Controversy*, ed. Sohan Modgil and Celia Modgil (Farmer, 1986), chapter 12.

64 For Damasio's analysis see Antonio Damasio, *Descartes' Error* (Vintage, 2006), pp. 34–51.

65 *"requires that"*: Joshua Greene and Jonathan Haidt, "How (and Where) Does Moral Judgment Work?," *TRENDS in Cognitive Science*, vol. 6, no. 12, 2002, p. 519; for the original study see Joshua Greene et al., "An fMRI Investigation of Emotional Engagement in Moral Judgment," *Science*, vol. 293, Sept. 14, 2001, pp. 2105–2108

65 *"We are born"*: Frans de Waal, *Our Inner Ape: A Leading Primatologist Describes Why We Are Who We Are* (New York, Penguin, 2005), p. 2.

66 *"immediate feeling"*: Quoted in Haidt, "The Emotional Dog," p. 816.

66 *"How selfish soever"*: Adam Smith, *The Theory of Moral Sentiments* (Book Jungle, 2007), pp. 1–2.

66 For the 2009 study see Sarina Rodrigues et al., "Oxytocin Receptor Genetic Variation Relates to Empathy and Stress Reactivity in Humans," *Proceedings of the National Academy of Sciences*, Nov. 23, 2009, accessed May 6, 2011, www.pnas.org/content/early/2009/11/18/0909579106.full.pdf+html.

67 *"greatest ruffian . . . brother"*: ASTM, pp. 1–2. On the distinction between Smith's and Hume's accounts of sympathy, see Samuel Fleischacker, "Hume and Smith on Sympathy: A Contrast, Critique and Reconstruction." I am indebted to Steven Lukes for sharing this paper with me.

69 *"is an exercise"*: Philip Gourevitch, *We Wish to Inform You That Tomorrow We Will Be Killed with Our Families: Stories from Rwanda* (Farrar, Straus and Giroux, 1998), pp. 95–96.

69 *"communal work . . . we celebrated"*: Philip Gourevitch, "The Life After," *The New Yorker*, May 4, 2009, pp. 40–41.

69 *"Man has . . . the latter."*: Erich Fromm, *Escape from Freedom* (Owl, 1994), pp. 18, 208.

75 *"black sheep . . . standing alone"*: Solomon Asch, "Studies of Independence and Conformity: I. A Minority of One Against a Unanimous Majority," *Psychological Monographs*, vol. 70, no. 9, 1956, pp. 31, 70.

76 For fMRI results and a description of the conformity experiment see Gregory S. Berns et al., "Neurobiological Correlates of Social Conformity and Independence During Mental Rotation," *Biological Psychiatry*, no. 58, 2005, pp. 245–53. Quotation acquired through personal interview.

77 *"All my patients suffered"*: David Homel, *The Speaking Cure* (Douglas and McIntyre, 2003), p. 6

80 *"No more arresting"*: Benedict Anderson, *Imagined Communities* (Verso, 1991), p. 9. For a discussion of nationalism not as political ideology see pp. 5–6.

81 *"Many mixed marriages"*: Glenny, *The Fall of Yugoslavia*, p. 90.

82 *"Are there . . . prevailing evil"*: Svetlana Broz, *Good People in an Evil Time*, trans. Ellen Elias-Bursać (Other, 2005), p. lxvii; for Zečar's story see pp. 119–22.

83 *"imagined communities . . . social interaction"*: Lynn Hunt, *Inventing Human Rights: A History* (Norton, 2007), pp. 32, 39.

3. THE RULES OF CONSCIENCE

85 *"Henry, if you"*: Walter Harding, *The Days of Henry Thoreau* (Princeton University Press, 1993), p. 199.

86 *"Under a government . . . right"*: Henry David Thoreau, *Collected Works* (Biblio Bazaar, 2008), pp. 30, 32, 35, 39, 45.

86 For Arendt on Thoreau see Hannah Arendt, *Crises of the Republic* (Mariner, 1972), pp. 58–68.

93 *"I don't have"*: Trudy Rubin, "The Siege of Beirut and the Reluctant Israeli Colonel," *Christian Science Monitor*, July 29, 1982.

94 *"Marines don't do"*: Mark Osiel, *Obeying Orders* (Transaction, 1999), p. 23.

95 *"unusually strong sense"*: Robert J. Lifton, *Home from the War: Vietnam Veterans; Neither Victims nor Executioners* (Simon & Schuster, 1973), p. 58.

95 *"not public education"*: Hugo Adam Bedau, *Civil Disobedience in Focus* (Routledge, 1991), p. 7.

96 *"oldest charge . . . its integrity"*: Arendt, *Crises of the Republic*, pp. 60–62.

98 *"If members of"*: Lassa Oppenheim, *International Law: A Treatise*, 3rd ed., vol. 1 (Lawbooks Exchange, 2005), p. 342.

99 *"if in obedience . . . punished"*: Matthew Lippman, "Humanitarian Law: The Development and Scope of the Superior Orders Defense," *Penn State International Law Review,* Fall 2001, pp. 174–75.

99 *"It was the"*: Osiel, *Obeying,* p. 58.

99 *"The fact that"*: United Nations, *Principles of International Law Recognized in the Charter of the Nürnberg Tribunal and in the Judgment of the Tribunal: 1950,* accessed May 10, 2011, untreaty.un.org/ilc/texts/instruments/english/draft%20articles/7_1_1950.pdf.

100 For details on the Kafr Qassem massacre see Dalia Karpel, "Do the Right Thing," *Ha'aretz,* Oct. 17, 2008.

101 *"What about women"*: ibid.

101 *"I did not"*: ibid.

102 *"The distinguishing mark"*: Osiel, *Obeying,* p. 77. Also see note 13, which shows that the Eichmann court quoted the ruling from the Kafr Qassem case.

107 *"If I knew"*: Harding, *Days of Henry Thoreau,* p. 302.

108 *"A man's . . . person"*: Michael Walzer, *Obligations: Essays on Disobedience, War, and Citizenship* (Harvard University Press, 1970), p. 122; Madison quoted on p. 125.

108 *"nobody ought to"*: John Locke, *A Letter Concerning Toleration* (Classic, 2009), p. 41.

109 *"I too recently"*: Yariv Oppenheimer, "Ma'ariv 'Soldiers Don't Issue Ultimatums' by Yariv Oppenheimer, Peace Now Secretary General," trans. Noam Shelef, Americans for Peace Now, Nov. 11, 2009.

116 *"The decision to"*: Ruth Linn, *Not Shooting and Not Crying: Psychological Inquiry into Moral Disobedience* (Greenwood, 1989), p. 57.

119 *"These were not"*: Ari Shavit, "The Big Freeze," *Ha'aretz,* Oct. 8, 2004.

120 For Levy's study on refusal see Yagil Levy, "The Embedded Military: Why Did the IDF Perform Effectively in Executing the Disengagement Plan?," *Security Studies,* vol. 16, no. 3, pp. 382–408.

120 *"Shimshon Does . . . eat it"*: Eyal Press, "Israel's Holy Warriors," *The New York Review of Books,* April 29, 2010.

121 *"We are . . . moral necessity"*: *Refusenik! Israel's Soldiers of Conscience,* ed. Peretz Kidron (Zed, 2004), pp. xii–xiii.

123 *"rules of . . . wrongdoer"*: Arendt, *Crises of the Republic,* pp. 62–63.

123 *"Why did this Hitler"*: Peter Braaksma, *Nine Lives: Making the Impossible Possible* (New Internationalist, 2009), p. 53.

124 *"by a rubber bullet"*: Chaim Levinson, "Court Holds State Responsible for Shooting of Palestinian Girl," *Ha'aretz,* Aug. 16, 2010.

126 *"Come take my picture"*: Tamar Yarom, *To See If I'm Smiling* (First Hand Films, 2007), 0:47.

4. THE PRICE OF RAISING ONE'S VOICE

131 This and other documents related to Leyla Wydler's case were obtained directly by the author.

132 *"It is like"*: Monica Perin, "International Investment," *Houston Business Journal*, vol. 30, no. 22, Oct. 22, 1999, p. 14.

133 For the relationship with SIB and CD offering see U.S. Securities and Exchange Commission, Office of Inspector General, *Investigation of the SEC's Response to Concerns Regarding Robert Allen Stanford's Alleged Ponzi Scheme*, Case No. OIG-526, March 31, 2010, pp. 29–31.

135 For the relationship with Kroll see William Finnegan, "The Secret Keeper: Jules Kroll and the World of Corporate Intelligence," *The New Yorker*, Oct. 19, 2009, and Matthew Goldstein, "Kroll's Roll in the Stanford Muck," *Reuters*, Sept. 11, 2009.

139 Details on bonuses of Stanford employees are drawn from the court-appointed receiver's application for a temporary restraining order or preliminary injunction concerning their accounts. See *Ralph S. Janvey v. James R. Alguire et al.*, Case No. 03-09-CV-0724-N, U.S. District Court for the Northern District of Texas, Dallas Division, filed April 19, 2010, pp. 6–7.

143 *"By risking everything"*: "Persons of the Year" Issue, *Time*, Dec. 30, 2002.

143 *"born, not made"*: Philip Jos, M. E. Tompkins, and S. W. Hayes, "In Praise of Difficult People," *Public Administration Review*, vol. 49, no. 6, p. 557.

143 *"Results indicate that"*: Randi Sims, "Collective Versus Individualist National Cultures: Comparing Taiwan and U.S. Employee Attitudes Toward Unethical Business Practices," *Business Society*, vol. 48, no. 1, March 2009.

146 *"the love of wealth"*: Alexis de Tocqueville, *Democracy in America*, trans. Henry Reeve (Edward Walker, 1847), p. 243.

147 *"Whistleblowers, we discovered"*: Myron Peretz Glazer and Penina Migdal Glazer, *The Whistleblowers: Exposing Corruption in Government & Industry* (Basic, 1989), pp. 5–6.

148 *"socially responsible personality"*: Jos et al., "In Praise," p. 557.

149 *"Voice is here"*: Albert Hirschman, *Exit, Voice, and Loyalty* (Harvard, 1970), p. 30.

150 *"The curious conformism"*: ibid., pp. 107–108.

150 For the *Times* exposé of police misconduct see David Burnham, "Graft

Paid to Police Here Said to Run into Millions," *New York Times*, Apr. 25, 1970.

150 *"I think it is time"*: Judith Ehrlich, *The Most Dangerous Man in America* (Ehrlich and Goldsmith, 2009).

152 *"In the United States"*: Roberta Ann Johnson, *Whistleblowing: When it Works—and Why* (Lynne Rienner, 2003), p. 20.

152 *"In general . . . get along"*: Claude Fischer, "Sweet Land of . . . Conformity? Americans Aren't the Rugged Individuals We Think We Are," *Boston Globe*, June 6, 2010.

153 *"criminal political backdealings"*: Ellen Nakashima, "Bradley Manning Is at the Center of the Wikileaks Controversy, but Who Is He?" *Washington Post*, May 4, 2011.

156 *"Among the . . . poorer"*: C. Fred Alford, *Whistleblowers: Broken Lives and Organizational Power* (Cornell, 2001), pp. 19–20, 110.

157 *"adverse and discriminatory"*: United States Department of Labor, *Welch v. Cardinal Bankshares Corp.*, Case No 2003-SOX-15 (Administrative Law Judges, 2004), p. 43.

158 *"the worst environmental"*: Barack Obama, "Remarks by the President to the Nation on the BP Oil Spill," Office of the Press Secretary, June 25, 2010.

159 *"often saw unsafe"*: Ian Urbina, "Workers on Doomed Rig Voiced Concern About Safety," *New York Times*, July 21, 2010.

159 *"Conformists are . . . crucial discussions"*: Cass Sunstein, *Why Societies Need Dissent* (Harvard, 2003), pp. 2–5.

160 *"By speaking the"*: Václav Havel, *The Power of the Powerless: Citizens Against the State in Central-Eastern Europe*, trans. Paul Wilson (Palach, 1985), p. 63.

160 For the Markopolos account see Harry Markopolos, *No One Would Listen: A Financial Thriller* (Fox Hounds, 2011).

162 *"A legal system"*: Sunstein, *Societies*, pp. 109–10.

162 *"seven years . . . prime mover"*: Alford, *Whistleblowers*, p. 53.

169 *"comprehensive and complete"*: U.S. Securities and Exchange Commission, p. 2.

170 *"If it . . . in you"*: Michael Sallah and Rob Barry, "Feds Probe Banker Allen Stanford's Ties to Congress," *Miami Herald*, Dec. 27, 2009. For more details on Stanford's political contributions and dealings in Antigua see also Bryan Burrough, "Pirate of the Caribbean," *Vanity Fair*, vol. 51, no. 7, July 2009.

171 *"absolutely ludicrous . . . of us"*: U.S. Securities and Exchange Commission, pp. 17–19, 54–56.

172 *"tire kicker . . . Ponzi scheme"*: U.S. Securities and Exchange Commission, pp. 64–70. See this section for additional details, including the SEC's jurisdictional issues.

EPILOGUE

177 *"Mr. Jawad's continued detention"*: Darrel Vandeveld, Written Statement of Darrel Vandeveld, "Exhibit B," Case 1:05-cv-02385-RMU, Jan. 12, 2009, accessed May 16, 2011, p. 14.

177 For more on Jawad's release see William Glaberson, "Judge Orders Guantánamo Detainee to Be Freed," *New York Times*, July 30, 2009.

177 *"no grounds"*: Lawrence Morris, "Guantánamo Prosecutor Is Quitting in Dispute Over a Case," *New York Times*, Sept. 24, 2008.

179 *"I became convinced"*: Martin Luther King, Jr., *The Autobiography of Martin Luther King, Jr.* (Warner, 2001), p. 14.

180 *"a merely personal moral"*: Supreme Court of the United States, *United States v. Seeger*, 380 U.S. 163, March 8, 1965.

180 *"a shared . . . certainly share"*: Michael Walzer, *Obligations: Essays on Disobedience, War, and Citizenship* (Harvard University Press, 1970), pp. 121, 130–31.

182 *"to fall out"*: Susan Sontag, *At the Same Time: Essays and Speeches* (Farrar, Straus and Giroux, 2007), p. 181.

ACKNOWLEDGMENTS

I have incurred many debts while writing this book, above all to the people in various countries and walks of life who entrusted me with their stories. For sharing their time and opening their lives to me, I am deeply grateful to them.

Many thanks to Aleksandar Opacic and Irfan Redzovic, who helped me navigate various language and logistical barriers during my travels through the Balkans. I also want to thank Ruth Dreifuss, who generously connected me to the right people in Switzerland. I have benefited from the assistance of Sara Sugihara, a superb translator who provided me with crucial assistance on chapter 1, and Neima Jahromi, a first-rate researcher who fact-checked the manuscript.

I am indebted to the late Tony Judt, a great historian and public intellectual who, early on, encouraged me to pursue this idea and provided me with invaluable advice, and to Steven Lukes for his incisive feedback on work in progress. I am equally grateful to my agent, Sarah Chalfant, who saw promise in this book long before it existed and steered it to the right home.

Special thanks to my editor at Farrar, Straus and Giroux, Eric Chinski, whose rigor, acumen, and erudition make it an honor to work with him. His scrupulous editing and expert guidance have immeasurably enriched my work. Thanks as well to Gabriella Doob, Katie Freeman, Susan Goldfarb, and many others at FSG who helped bring this book to fruition.

Several institutions provided critical support along the way, among them the Open Century Project at Central European University, where I spent six valuable months. Particular thanks go to Ivona Malbasic, Ivan Krastev, and Jair Kessler at the affiliated Remarque Institute of New York University. I would like to acknowledge the New America Foundation, a vibrant institution where I have been a fellow, and especially Andrés Martinez, Sherle Schwenninger, and Steve Coll. Thanks also to the Nation Institute, which generously made a workspace available to me, and particularly to Katrina vanden Heuvel, Ruth Baldwin, Marissa Colon-Margolies, Taya Kitman, Carl Bromley, and Andy Breslau.

I am grateful to various friends and colleagues for their humor, wise counsel, and support, above all Peter Yost, Adam Shatz, Laura Secor, Sasha Abramsky, Ta'Nehisi Coates, Chase Madar, Satish Moorthy, Scott Sherman, John Palattella, Eric Klinenberg, Kirk Semple, Steve Dudley, David Gartner, Johnny Temple, Toby Beach, Benjamin Yost, Ari Berman, Christian Parenti, and Lila Azam Zanganeh.

I would like to thank my parents and my sister, Sharon, for their unflagging love and support, and the members of my extended family, in particular my aunt Talma, my cousins Lior and Yaron, and Ernst Abelin, Graciela Abelin-Sas Rose, and Gilbert Rose. My deepest gratitude goes to Mireille Abelin. Her love sustains me, and her wisdom, courage, and compassion inspire me.